TRANSFORMATIVE CIVIC ENGAGEMENT THROUGH COMMUNITY ORGANIZING

TRANSFORMATIVE CIVIC ENGAGEMENT THROUGH COMMUNITY ORGANIZING

Maria Avila

Foreword by Scott J. Peters

Afterword by Michael Gecan

STERLING, VIRGINIA

Published by Stylus Publishing, LLC.
22883 Quicksilver Drive
Sterling, Virginia 20166-2102

Library of Congress Cataloging-in-Publication Data

Names: Avila, Maria, 1955- author.
Title: Transformative civic engagement through community
organizing / Maria Avila ; foreword by Scott Peters ;
afterword by Michael Gecan.
Description: Sterling, Virginia : Stylus Publishing, LLC, 2018. |
Includes bibliographical references.
Identifiers: LCCN 2017023005 (print) |
LCCN 2017047644 (ebook) |
ISBN 9781620361054 (Library networkable e-edition) |
ISBN 9781620361061 (Consumer e-edition) |
ISBN 9781620361047 (pbk. : alk. paper) |
ISBN 9781620361030 (cloth : alk. paper)
Subjects: LCSH: Community organization--Study and teaching
(Higher) | Transformative learning. | Community and college. |
Democracy and education.
Classification: LCC HM766 (ebook) | LCC HM766 .A85 2018
(print) | DDC 378.1/03--dc23
LC record available at https://lccn.loc.gov/2017023005

13-digit ISBN: 978-1-62036-103-0 (cloth)
13-digit ISBN: 978-1-62036-104-7 (paperback)
13-digit ISBN: 978-1-62036-105-4 (library networkable e-edition)
13-digit ISBN: 978-1-62036-106-1 (consumer e-edition)

Printed in the United States of America

All first editions printed on acid-free paper
that meets the American National Standards Institute
Z39-48 Standard.

Bulk Purchases

Quantity discounts are available for use in workshops and for
staff development.
Call 1-800-232-0223

First Edition, 2018

10   9   8   7   6   5   4   3   2   1

To my husband, Dave, with gratitude for patiently listening and for lovingly holding me through my ups and downs while writing this book.

To my nieces, Paty and Diana, and their children, Fernando, Itxayana, Paulina, and Alitzel.

CONTENTS

FOREWORD

A friend who is a professor at a large public research university called me up 10 years or so ago, eager to tell me a story. "You have to hear this," he said. "I just got out of a meeting where I made some points about our responsibilities—both collectively as an institution and individually as scholars—to advance democracy. After it was over, a senior administrator pulled me aside. 'I heard what you said,' he told me, 'but with all due respect, we don't do democracy. We create knowledge, and we disseminate it. *Government* does democracy.'"

My friend and I laughed at first. Then we got angry. In the years since, we've both come to use this story's punchline—*We don't do democracy*—as a sobering reminder of what academic professionals who want to engage in the work of democracy are up against.

It would be hard to come up with a better line than "We don't do democracy" to capture the exact opposite of Maria Avila's core message in this remarkable book. Her core message isn't that we already "do democracy" in higher education. Rather, it's that we can and should. Importantly, she doesn't deliver this message as a theoretical model, or a moral or ideological argument. She develops it as a set of inquiry-based insights, achieved through critically reflective interpretations of stories about her own work and experience. While the stories are uniquely her own, the insights she draws from them have broad application. They open our imagination to new possibilities, even as they also reveal new and difficult challenges.

The possibilities and challenges this book reveals are tied to a distinctive way of answering what I think of as higher education's public purposes and work question (Peters, 2010). As a historian who uses conceptual tools from development sociology, narrative inquiry, and political theory to study American higher education, I'm aware of how deeply contested answers to that question have been and continue to be. The senior administrator's comments in the story with which I opened this foreword reflect one answer: Our public purpose and work are not to "do democracy" but rather to create and disseminate knowledge. Based on a government-centered view of democracy, this answer makes some sense. But it also has several problems. It leaves out the long-standing role of social criticism that has been performed for centuries by scholars in (and beyond) the arts and humanities.

It begs an important question: What kinds of knowledge does a society that professes or aspires to be "democratic" need, and where, how, by whom, and to what ends is such knowledge created, produced, discovered, tested, communicated, and used? And perhaps most importantly, it reflects a narrow understanding of what democracy is, and who "does" it.

To fully appreciate and make sense of Avila's book, we must recognize that her answer to the public purposes and work question is grounded in a broad people-centered rather than narrow government-centered view of democracy. A broad view of democracy has deep roots in American history, including higher education. For example, we find it in a passage from the Highlander Folk School's statement of purpose, drafted in the mid-1950s by civil rights leader Septima Clark, which speaks of "broadening the scope of democracy to include everyone and deepening the concept to include every relationship" (quoted in Payne, 1995/2007, p. 68). And we find it in the writings of the pragmatist philosopher John Dewey (1937), who argued that democracy "has to be enacted anew in every generation, in every year and day, in the living relations of person to person in all social forms and institutions" (p. 237). That includes institutions of higher education, as President Truman's Commission on Higher Education proclaimed in its 1947 report when it wrote that the "first and most essential charge upon higher education is that at all its levels and in all its fields of specialization it shall be the carrier of democratic values, ideals, and processes" (President's Commission on Higher Education, p. 102).

Avila doesn't merely embrace and proclaim this "first and most essential charge" in this book. She teaches us a set of practices that we can use to enact it, drawn and adapted from her long career as a broad-based community organizer: one-to-one meetings, collective leadership development, power and interest mapping, and ongoing reflection that is both critical and collective. These practices can enliven and humanize our engagement work, and keep us from turning it into deadly, dehumanizing, formulaic programs. Used well they help us open spaces and paths for learning, theory building, and knowledge making that are highly complex and transdisciplinary (which, by the way, most of our pressing issues and problems are as well). They help us turn the naming and framing of issues and problems and the development and implementation of strategies for action to address them into a deliberative *civic* rather than expert-dominated technical task. And they enable us to pursue a key public purpose: the discovery, development, and strengthening of civic leadership, capacities, agency, and power—individual and collective—for long-term rather than episodic work. In short, they offer higher education a way to "do democracy," in the living relations of person to person, at all its levels and in all its fields of specialization.

I can't end this foreword without acknowledging the difficulty of not only taking up but also sustaining the practices Avila teaches us in this book. They require skills that are rarely taught and rewarded, in and beyond academia. They're time consuming. And they're radically countercultural, not only in every sector, discipline, and field of American higher education but also in our off-campus communities. They represent a distinctive kind of politics that stands in sharp contrast to—and cuts against the grain of—several more common varieties, such as feel-good service pursued through selfless acts of voluntarism; partisan, righteous, Manichean battles of good versus evil pursued through activist protests and mobilizations; and technocratic treatments of social "sicknesses" (e.g., childhood obesity) pursued through the scripted implementation of evidence-based programs. My point here—and I think Avila's point in this book as well—is not that other varieties of politics are categorically bad or wrong, always and everywhere. They aren't. Rather, it's that the relational, developmental, public work politics that her four practices represent enable us to pursue and achieve things the other varieties can't.

To say the practices Avila teaches us in this book are countercultural doesn't mean they don't connect with things that are in our culture, in and out of academia. There are people everywhere who already use one or more of them, regardless of whether they name or think of their work as having anything to do with democracy or politics. And everywhere there is an underlying hunger for ways to be engaged in productive, effective, meaningful, and satisfying public work with others.

In conclusion, I want to stress the meaningful and satisfying dimensions. What Avila is offering us here gives us ways to enhance not only the effectiveness of our work but also its *joyfulness*. As Carol Bebelle—cofounder and executive director of the Ashé Cultural Arts Center in New Orleans (www.ashecac.org/main/), and an Imagining America colleague of both mine and Avila's—beautifully teaches, doing democracy is or can be a way of *conjugating freedom*. That's a joyful, beautiful, and powerful act. Or at least it can be.

Avila's book, a gift to us all, can help us learn how to make it so.

Scott J. Peters
Professor of Development Sociology,
Cornell University
Faculty Codirector (2012–2017), Imagining America:
Artists and Scholars in Public Life

ACKNOWLEDGMENTS

There is a very long list of friends and colleagues who have been part of my journey as an organizer and as an academic, and who had significant roles in the genesis and development of this book. I start by thanking all of my colleagues in the Industrial Areas Foundation (IAF), but especially Dick Harmond for his bold, agitational, yet loving and supportive mentoring. Dick, you got me started with this life long process of engaging with my narrative—my birthright.

I thank all of my colleagues at Occidental College, whose collaborative leadership cocreated the Center for Community-Based Learning (CCBL) and the Northeast Education Strategies Group (NESG). There were many such colleagues. They include Elizabeth Chin, Peter Drier, Regina Freer, Bob Gottlieb, Felisa Guillen, Kathy Harrison, Surya Kalra, Alan Knoerr, Donna Maeda, Martha Matsuoka, Ricardo Mireles, Alexis Moreno, Maria Lorena Nunez, Nik Orlando, and Ref Rodriguez.

A special thank you to the many civic engagement pioneers who guided me in what, at the time I started the CCBL, was new and unknown territory. Among these colleagues are Harry Boyte, Dick Cone, and Amy Driscoll. A special thank you to Amy, who guided me in submitting the contract for this book.

In Ireland, I am indebted to so many friends and colleagues who made it possible for me to study outside of the United States and who invested in my development as an academic researcher. They include Tom Collins, Brid Connolly, Shauna Gilligan, Seamus Lillis, Saranne Magennis, Lorraine McIlrath, and Anne Ryan.

At the University of Southern California (USC), I thank all of the faculty, staff, and community partners who were part of my postdoctoral research. Among them, George Sanchez was (and still is) a significant influence in my development as an academic-in-training, through my postdoctoral fellowship under his mentorship.

In Imagining America (IA), I am grateful to the faculty, administrators, community partners, and students who have been part of my development as a national academic organizer. I am especially grateful to Scott J. Peters for his patient, tireless commitment to my journey as a writer. I am equally grateful to the rest of the IA team: Kevin Bott, Tim Eatman, Jamie Haft, and Holly Zahn.

At the Kettering Foundation, I am grateful to Derek Barker for his ability to make sense of my organizing work and thus turn it into collaborative research partnerships with the foundation. He did this with my postdoc at USC and with my democratic engagement project at the California State University, Dominguez Hills (CSUDH).

At CSUDH, I thank my colleagues, students, and community partners who participated in my democratic engagement project, and my colleagues in the Master of Social Work department. I especially thank my chair, Mekada Graham, for being a thinking partner through the writing of this book.

Last but not least, I am grateful to John von Knorring, my editor, for his guidance and encouragement. Many thanks, too, to the blind reviewers for their detailed comments on an early draft of this book.

I

INTRODUCTION AND
OVERVIEW

[T]he dominant paradigm of civic engagement in higher education does
not express or actively seek to fulfill a democratic purpose, and . . . colleges and universities, in the absence of this larger sense of purpose for
civic engagement work, have failed to pursue the kind of institutional
change needed to realign the central premise and core work of the academy.
(Saltmarsh & Hartley, 2012, p. 1)

I am a community organizer engaged in and committed to creating a culture in which higher education can fulfill a larger democratic purpose
through civically engaged scholarship. In this type of culture, the various
stakeholders within higher education will create spaces where they, engaged
with off-campus stakeholders, can cocreate and enact a democratic purpose
for their campus and surrounding communities. In this scenario, the interests, knowledge, and resources of all parties involved will be the basis for civically engaged projects and partnerships. This reciprocal process can then lead
to creating institutional change in higher education, communities surrounding colleges and universities, and society at large. Furthermore, this process
will be based on intentionally building individual and collective civic agency.

In this book, I present an approach through which community organizing
can help create a civically engaged, democratic culture inside and outside colleges and universities, by cocreating collective leadership, and I do this by
sharing the processes and results of my work of over a decade. This approach
to civic engagement is different from dominant approaches that are based on
opportunities for student volunteerism and from approaches based on faculty
providing technical assistance to communities. These different approaches
are often transactional, short term, and project specific, in ways that all too
often exclude long-lasting human and community development. My point,
however, is not to condemn any civic engagement modalities, and I know

1

from experience that the ideal reciprocal engagement I am presenting here is not always possible for a variety of reasons. I recognize, too, that the community organizing approach I offer here is not the only way to create institutional and societal change, but it is one I have been experimenting with in various local, national, and international contexts. Therefore, writing this book is a way for me not only to synthesize the lessons I have learned but also to recognize the many faculty members, administrators, students, and community partners who have been part of my work.

My organizing work in higher education has focused primarily on working with faculty who are interested in creating this type of culture within their institutions and working on this endeavor along with other relevant stakeholders, such as their faculty colleagues, administrators, students, and community partners. My interest in working primarily with faculty stems from experiential and empirical knowledge that they have the potential to create this type of culture, much more than students or administrators do, in part because faculty tend to stay the longest at their institutions. I know that many faculty members are already civically engaged scholars, but I also know that in many cases they are not doing this with the intent of creating institutional culture change, and they are not doing it as part of a collective. In fact, in many cases, civically engaged scholarship has offered faculty a way to escape institutional conditions where they do not feel valued and supported. The approach I am presenting here first evolved at Occidental College in Los Angeles, where I was founding director of the Center for Community-Based Learning (CCBL) from 2001 to 2011.

I have explored the community organizing approach I used at Occidental at other higher education institutions, particularly through my doctoral research at Maynooth University in Ireland (2009–2012) and postdoctoral research at the University of Southern California (USC) in Los Angeles (2012–2014). In addition, I have explored this approach at the national level in the United States through various roles I have played with Imagining America (IA)—a national consortium of more than 100 higher education institutions involved in advancing publicly engaged scholarship that draws on arts, humanities, and design—and through collaborative research projects with the Kettering Foundation. The most recent of these projects took place at California State University, Dominguez Hills (CSUDH), in Los Angeles, from 2015 to 2016, in my role as tenure-track faculty in the master of social work program.

Through these various projects I have learned that civically engaged scholarship, although practiced at most institutions in the United States and in many other countries, is not generally supported, valued, or rewarded. I have also learned that a significant reason for this is that higher education, like most other public sectors in society, has lost significant financial support.

One consequence of this loss is that higher education is relying on a business model in which education is transactional, and thus not conducive to a culture that values civically engaged scholarship. Related to this business model is a pattern that has become familiar to those of us working in higher education; namely, the short time administrators tend to stay at a given institution, often driven by an interest in career advancement. Students, too, tend to see a college education as a ticket to well-paying jobs—another form of careerism.

Many point to the success of the market and the integration of its values and practices into all or most sectors of society as a significant driver for this business model that many colleges and universities are seemingly following. Rather than focusing on lamenting such conditions, I argue that it is important to understand this reality. In organizing terms this means *understanding the world as it is*, which is necessary in order to come up with strategies that can help us create spaces where various stakeholders can dialogue and deliberate about what higher education's democratic mission could and should be. Cocreating a vision of what this democratic mission could and should be would be part of *creating the world as we would like it to be*, to use another community organizing phrase. Integrating community organizing practices into civic engagement work—particularly reciprocal, cocreative, and relational civically engaged scholarship—is one strategy for creating the world as we would like it to be. This argument is based on the well-known fact that knowledge produced in higher education already has a major influence in societies throughout the world. Thus, a higher education sector with this type of cocreated civically engaged democratic mission is then likely to enhance democratic societies. I illustrate how this can take place by using examples from my community organizing, civic engagement work in several contexts and institutions.

The Origins of My Community Organizing Work in Higher Education

I aspired to bring my organizing practice into my civic engagement work at Occidental, but this became clear only within the first year of developing what CCBL's charge would be. Three events and three people played a significant role in bringing this realization to me. First, I met Dick Cone shortly after he had retired as director of the Joint Education Project (JEP) at USC. The JEP is a civic engagement–related center that recently celebrated its fortieth anniversary. Cone told me that he was intrigued by my organizing background and how I was approaching civic engagement. He suggested that I attend an upcoming national civic engagement conference. Before long, I received an invitation to this conference to present about my work at Occidental. Second, after the conference, I met with Ted Mitchell, at the time Occidental's president, and shared my presentation with him. I asked him to give me feedback. When the CCBL was founded, it was housed under the president's office; therefore, meeting with him was not unusual. Mitchell said that he could see that I was using my community organizing training to develop the work of the CCBL, and he seemed to like this. The third event happened the following year. I attended another civic engagement conference, where Harry Boyte, at the time codirector of the Center for Democracy and Citizenship at the University of Minnesota, was a panel presenter. In his presentation, Boyte spoke about his organizing work at his center, and after his presentation I spoke with him. Boyte became a friend and a mentor in further integrating community organizing into my civic engagement work at Occidental, and he has continued to play an important role throughout the years.

My community organizing approach to civic engagement is an adaptation of what I learned as an organizer with the Industrial Areas Foundation (IAF) from 1990 to 2000, in New Mexico; Los Angeles, California; and northern California. The IAF was founded by the late Saul Alinsky in 1940 in Chicago, and its purpose is to build broad-based organizations through which member institutions, such as places of worship, unions, and schools, can learn how to obtain and practice relational power to create positive societal change (Alinsky, 1969, 1971; Chambers, 2003; Gecan, 2002; Osterman, 2002; Rogers, 1990). The IAF has chapters in many states in the United States, as well as in other countries, such as Australia, England, Germany, and Canada.

As this approach to civic engagement was evolving at Occidental, I became interested in whether this type of civic engagement could be replicated in other institutions. This led me to pursue a PhD. I did my doctoral studies in adult and community education at Maynooth University (formerly National University of Maynooth) in Ireland from 2009 to 2012. My research focused on exploring whether the approach I used at Occidental could work at Maynooth to build a movement that would interest academics and administrators in institutionalizing civically engaged scholarship. I interviewed faculty, administrators, and community partners, exploring their views and experiences on civically engaged teaching and research and on the role the university can play in their surrounding region.

After graduation from Maynooth, I started an Andrew Mellon postdoctoral fellowship at USC. There, from 2012 to 2014, I interviewed faculty and community partners around the same themes I used at Maynooth. During this time, I also became part of a national project led by IA that explored whether other higher education institutions would be interested in using community organizing through their civic engagement work. My role was to codesign and cofacilitate one national summer organizing institute in 2013 in Los Angeles, California and another one in Atlanta, Georgia in 2014. These institutes were attended by participants from various colleges and universities, including faculty, administrators, community partners, and graduate students. I was invited to join IA's National Advisory Board in 2015, and in this capacity, I began organizing an IA regional cluster in southern California later that year.

In connection with my postdoctoral research and my work with IA since 2009 I have collaborated in several research workshops and projects with the Kettering Foundation. For example, the foundation funded the second year of my postdoctoral research on civic engagement at USC. In addition, it funded a research project, also on civic engagement in 2015–2016, at CSUDH, through my role as tenure-track faculty in the Master of Social Work program. The foundation's research collaborations with academics from various higher education institutions aim to explore and experiment with ways in which faculty scholarship can contribute to increasing citizen participation in solving problems that affect them and their communities. This stems from the foundation's research question: What does it take to make democracy work as it should?

Throughout my work with these various institutions and projects, I have gained valuable lessons as I have built from one experience to another, as well as from the diversity of types of institutions and organizations. For example, Occidental is a small (around 2,000 students), private, liberal arts, residential college; Maynooth is a public, medium-sized (about 9,000 students) institution, and it increasingly resembles a research type of university; and USC is a large (over 40,000 students), private research university. IA, in contrast, has given me the opportunity to learn about the national state of higher education regarding civically engaged scholarship.

Civic Engagement as a Movement That Aims to Realize a Larger Purpose for Higher Education

My approach to civic engagement was influenced by conversations with many scholars and practitioners of the civic engagement movement I met at conferences in the early 2000s (e.g., Dick Cone, Harry Boyte, Barbara Holland, Nadine Cruz, and Amy Driscoll). In these conversations many of these pioneers of the movement said that civic engagement (at the time referred to mostly as *service-learning*) had not accomplished what many of them saw as its original intent. This original intent, as discussed by several authors, was to enhance the social responsibility of college students during and after their college education through courses in all disciplines. Thus, Campus Compact (2016a), an organization that has promoted service-learning and civic engagement for decades, states on its website that its mission is to advance "the public purposes of colleges and universities by deepening their ability to improve community life and to educate students for civic and social responsibility."

This intent came in response to what many have described as a predominant civic disengagement and the role that higher education should play in reversing this disengagement. Colby and Ehrlich (2000) affirm this in the introduction to the book *Civic Responsibility and Higher Education*:

> The essays in this volume are rooted in the common concerns of the authors about the increasing public disdain for civic engagement, particularly political involvement, in this country, and their common beliefs that higher education should have important roles in reversing those trends. (p. xxi)

This contemporary attempt to connect higher education with social problems, however, is not new.

One such attempt can be traced back to 1862, during President Lincoln's administration and in response to Congressman Justin Smith Morrill's advocacy for farmers, who at the time were the overwhelming majority of the national population (Cantor, 2012). Former chancellor and president of Syracuse University Nancy Cantor writes that the Morrill Act "launched a revolution in higher education by providing for what would become known as 'democracy's colleges'. [These colleges] were aimed simultaneously at spreading innovation through university-community collaboration and fostering access to education for the next generation of farmers" (p. 2).

Adding to this historical event, in his book *Democracy and Higher Education: Traditions and Stories of Civic Engagement*, Scott Peters (2010) offers a more recent perspective, based on a report from a commission appointed by President Harry S. Truman in 1947. This commission, states Peters, was charged with examining "the functions of higher education in our democracy and the means by which they can best be performed" (p. 4). Peters comments that the commission's report included higher education's off-campus engagement, thus indicating that higher education has a role in a free and democratic society, and that it must cease to be campus bound.

Connecting higher education's purpose with societal problems has never been a coherent, clearly defined, or understood movement, however, and the dissatisfaction expressed by many in the early 2000s is still present today. To this effect, John Saltmarsh and Matthew Hartley (2012) offer a critical analysis of civic engagement in their book *To Serve a Larger Purpose: Engagement for Democracy and the Transformation of Higher Education*. The authors' analysis is founded on Ernest Boyer's (1996) call for higher education to serve a larger purpose in the 1990s:

But, at a deeper level, I have this growing conviction that what's . . . needed is not just more programs, but a larger purpose, a larger sense of mission, a larger clarity of direction in the Nation's life . . . creating a special climate in which academic and civic cultures communicate more continuously and creatively with each other. (Boyer, p.1; cited in Saltmarsh & Hartley, 2012, pp. 32–33)

Saltmarsh and Hartley (2012) argue that Boyer's call for engagement goes beyond creating new programs; it is about a larger sense of mission in connection to the nation's life, and in communication with civic cultures, that has not yet been fully achieved by higher education. In this current state of civic engagement, the authors argue that

innovative practices that shift epistemology, reshape the curriculum, alter pedagogy, and redefine scholarship are not being supported through academic norms and institutional reward policies that shape change that occurs institutionally, and the civic engagement work appears to have been accommodated to the dominant expert-centered framework. Democratic engagement is not embedded in the institutional culture. It remains a marginalized activity, and its sustainability is questionable. (p. 33)

While Cantor's and Peters's reminder that there have been historical shifts in the understanding of what higher education's public mission should be is important, Saltmarsh and Hartley's analysis of the current state of civic engagement regarding its purpose, goals, and methodologies is an urgent call for action. Their analysis is a reminder that civic engagement is still not addressing the larger purpose that Boyer hoped for. This is not to say that there are not many cases of civic engagement accomplishments, as articulated by so many authors (Benson, Harkavy, & Puckett, 2007; Boyte, 2004; Cress & Donahue, 2011; Fear, Rosaen, Bawden, & Foster-Fishman, 2006; Koritz & Sanchez, 2009; Maurrasse, 2001; McIlrath, Lyons, & Munck, 2012; Peters, 2010; Stanton, Giles, & Cruz, 1999; Stoecker & Tryon, 2009; Strand, Marullo, Cutforth, Stoecker, & Donohue, 2003; Zlotkowski, 1998), but these accomplishments rarely include transforming the culture of higher education institutions and the regions where they exist in the way Boyer hoped for. As displayed on the websites of many universities' and colleges' civic engagement programs, thousands of college students are involved in projects such as tutoring low-income students in public schools; working with the homeless; effecting economic community development; and participating in electoral, political projects. Per my research and practice, however, many civic engagement projects are not created reciprocally with the organizations with which they partner so that interests, resources, and knowledge of the students (faculty if the projects are academically based) and the community partners are clearly and intentionally addressed. Equally important, many of these projects do not, in general, intentionally and clearly address the power disconnect between universities and colleges and their community partners.

What Saltmarsh and Hartley refer to in Boyer's previous quote, "larger clarity of direction in the Nation's life . . . creating a special climate in which academic and civic cultures communicate more continuously and creatively with each other," has to do with the culture of higher education and of society at large. These are challenges that require continuous, creative, educational, and challenging conversations between campus and off-campus stakeholders. In addition, understanding the national context for the parts of higher education's culture that we need to change requires us to understand the larger global economic forces affecting our nation, including neoliberalism. It also requires an awareness that these global forces are often intentionally organized by those who advocate for a free market society, and that they have an effect on how institutions operate, including higher education institutions (Brown, 2005; Peters & Avila, 2014).

The Market and Its Effect in Democratic Societies and in Higher Education

Wendy Brown (2005) writes that it is common to refer to the current regime in the United States as *neoconservative*. According to Brown, the neoconservative principles

> increase US global hegemony, dismantle the welfare state, retrench civil liberties, eliminate the right to abortion and affirmative action, re-Christianize the state, deregulate corporations, gut environmental protections, reverse progressive taxation, reduce education spending while reducing prison budgets, and feather the nest of the rich while criminalizing the poor. (p. 37)

While not disagreeing with this scenario, Brown (2005) aims to focus on what she calls our predicament "in terms of a neoliberal political rationality," which to her is more important than political stands on particular issues. Such rationality has emerged as a way of government not just in the state, and it results in "forms of citizens and behaviors, and a new organization of the social" (p. 37). This rationality has become part of the culture of democratic societies and their various institutions.

Irish scholar Kathleen Lynch (2008) comments on what this neoliberal political rationality has done to higher education: "Over the last decades

. . . universities have been transformed increasingly into powerful consumer-oriented corporate networks, whose public interest values have been seriously challenged" (p. 1). She adds,

> What is happening in the universities is that they are being asked to produce commercially oriented professionals rather than public-interest professionals (Hanlon, 2000). . .. The danger with this advancing marketised individualism is that it will further weaken public interest values among those who are university educated. Yet a welfare-oriented democratic state depends on the realization of such values to provide services on a universal basis. Without adhesion to such values, the only basis on which services will be provided is on the ability to pay. (pp. 2–3)

U.S. political theorist Sheldon Wolin's (1989) essay on contract and birthright offers an analysis that expands on Lynch's comments, but he does this referring to the implications of what he sees as a U.S. contract-based society. This contract-based society, he states, has been influenced by contract theory, which

> conceives of political society as the creation of individuals who freely consent to accept the authority and rules of political society on the basis of certain stipulated conditions, such as each shall be free to do as he or she pleases as long as his or her actions do not interfere with the rights of others; or that an individual shall not be deprived of property except by laws that have been passed by duly elected representatives; and so on. The contractual element is needed, according to the theory, because all persons being free and equal by nature and society being by nature in need of coercive power to protect rights, and preserve peace, and defend against external invasion, the freedom of individuals will have to be limited and regulated. Individuals will contract, therefore, to surrender some part of their rights in exchange for the protection of the law and the defense of society from foreign or domestic enemies. (pp. 138–139)

The rights that we have surrendered, according to Wolin, represent our politicalness, which to him is something we are born with. Based on this view, our politicalness is our birthright. By *politicalness* Wolin means "our capacity for developing into beings who know and value what it means to participate in and be responsible for the care and improvement of our common and collective life" (p. 139).

I interpret Wolin's definition of *politicalness* for my public scholarship and organizing work to mean that our birthright is about the rights and responsibilities with which we were born; to preserve and even improve the society we inherited for ourselves, those we love, and future generations.

This concept of our human legacy is the foundation of a democratic society, and hence Wolin (1989) calls us to create a vision for a society with a nonco-optable politics. "This means," as he sees it, "different actors, different scales of power, and different criteria of success" (p. 50) than what we now have. Above all, he believes that democracy needs a different type of participation than simply "'taking part,' as in elections or office holding. It means originating or initiating cooperative action with others" (p. 50). Wolin sees that in doing this in response to issues that affect us as a society "the political can become incorporated in the everyday lives of countless people" (p. 150). Or put in international scholar Harry Boyte's (2004) terms, this means that we as members of society become cocreators and political actors in our everyday routines.

Recovering this historical democratic, public mission of higher education through a culture that values and rewards civically engaged scholarship is central to this book. I am, however, compelled to comment about an assumption that we often make regarding the role that civic, nonprofit organizations can also play in enhancing the democracy. It is true that there is a significant resources and power gap between universities and colleges and the organizations with whom they partner. However, this recognition of inequality can easily turn into demonizing higher education institutions and idealizing (even victimizing) civic, nonprofit organizations. However, the contract-based society in which we have surrendered our rights as political beings referred to by Wolin affects these types of organizations as well. In addition, these types of organizations also have knowledge, power, and resources that can be combined with those from colleges and universities with whom they partner. This type of acknowledgment and understanding of resources, knowledge, and power that all stakeholders bring to campus-community partnerships is central to creating mutually beneficial, reciprocal partnerships. It is also important to acknowledge that because the two types of societal sectors have different cultures, calendars, ways of communicating, and reward systems, achieving this level of reciprocity requires significant effort, at least at the beginning. It is wise and beneficial to all stakeholders involved in civic engagement to keep this reality in mind, and for us to integrate it in the context of the type of civically engaged higher education institutions we aim to create.

The state of our democratic society, thus, is the larger context in which higher education operates as a sector. These are clearly not conditions in which the movement of civic engagement can succeed in influencing the direction of the national life. Therefore, civic engagement must have a strong focus on changing the culture of higher education and revitalizing its public mission, and not on creating outreach activities and programs, as mentioned in Boyer's quote. It is in this context of the state of democracy inside and outside higher education institutions that community organizing can create new spaces where the "cooperative action with others" that Wolin writes about can be originated, and where the institutional policies that reward the shifts in scholarship that Saltmarsh and Hartley call for can be pursued.

Collective Civic Agency

The process for creating this type of culture change is slow and intentional, and finding those who can commit to intentionally using their individual and collective civic agency requires a great deal of patience. Harry Boyte (2009) defines *civic agency* as "self-organizing, collective citizen efforts to solve problems and create public things in open settings without tight prior scripts" (p. 1). Boyte continues with the following:

> A civic agency approach is built through what we call public work, based on a sense of the citizen as a cocreator of a democratic way of life and a view that emphasizes politics' productive as well as participatory and distributive aspects. Such an approach is an alternative to conventional ideological politics, on the one hand, and community service and volunteerism, on the other. An alternative with rich emergent practices and concepts, it intimates the fulfillment of the vision of humanizing an impersonal world. (p. 1)

Boyte further makes the argument that we live in a society where academics are viewed as the ultimate knowledge holders, and he calls this "the cult of the expert" (p. 1). This cult of academic expertise makes it difficult to create reciprocal campus-university partnerships between academics and nonacademics as cocreators of a new society.

Given this scenario, we need to relearn, as individuals, institutions, communities, and a society, a new way of doing politics; we need to educate ourselves about the art of public life. Doing this requires that we as individuals reflect on and understand our birthright as civic agents, and it requires that we collectively figure out how to do this in the context of the market culture that predominates in our institutions and in society. Furthermore, we need to start small, include all relevant stakeholders, and be selective of those we invite to begin this important task. This can be started by aiming to create small spaces where this takes place, as opposed to aiming to change the entire culture of the institutions where we work. Because this type of change requires partners in and outside of academia, creating such spaces is important for nonacademic institutions and organizations as well.

Only by creating these spaces in our institutions and in our communities can the political become part of everyday life, to use another one of Boyte's concepts. I believe this is possible within all sectors of society, because the daunting problems faced by humanity today affect everyone at various levels, including those who work in the business sector and in government. I have been building such spaces throughout my community organizing work with the IAF since the 1990s and in higher education since 2001. I also have worked on short-term consulting projects with government and elected official offices. I am not alone in this work, and while institutions and communities cannot be transformed overnight, progress has been visible and palpable often within months of sustained organizing in all the arenas in which I have participated. This is what I strongly believe, from experience, that community organizing has the potential to do. But long-term, sustainable work must start from our personal narratives.

Organizing for change is deeply rooted in being in touch with our purpose in life. The late Brazilian adult educator Paulo Freire (1995) talks about the importance of reflecting on our historical reality as a way to develop our power to understand the way we exist, in order to transform ourselves and our world. Anne B. Ryan (2001), an Irish adult educator, explains that women often go through a journey of personal, critical reflection to find their way into political action for social justice. The late Cherokee chief Wilma Mankiller (1993) said in her biography that some Native American nations have a tradition of approaching social problems by reflecting on what related to this problem seven generations back, then engaging in creating a vision of what could be, seven generations forward. This is how certain they were of the importance of their past, present, and future stories, through which they reminded themselves of their inherited rights and responsibilities to enhance their communities. As IAF organizers, we learned that in order to be effective in building collectives of leaders we needed to be grounded in our own stories—the origin of our organizing work to create change in the world. Only then, we learned, could we help others act on their own stories. This type of critical reflection on an ongoing basis always feeds my soul, and it also reminds me of where I come from and why organizing is important to me. Critical reflection grounds me.

Learning through our narratives and through narrative interviews, which will be a significant part of this book, fits within participatory practices to create social change, as discussed by Margaret Ledwith and Jane Springett (2010). The authors of *Participatory Practice: Community-Based Action for Transformative Change* write that in their book they

> emphasise the use of story as a way of anchoring the process of change in lived experience. True to this approach, we shape aspects of our own story with you here. A participatory approach calls for us to acknowledge the ways in which our own life experiences have shaped the ideas that we share

with you, and these vignettes give you insight into critical moments that have influenced our theory and practice over the years. (p. 1)

They conceive of participatory practice as ontological and transformational for us as academics and organizers, with implications for our work to transform society and the world. It is in this context that I share the evolution of my organizing work in higher education throughout this book. This is also the context in which I share excerpts from narrative interviews I conducted with faculty, administrators, students, and community partners, particularly in chapters 3 and 4. These interviews were spaces where those I interviewed and I engaged in participatory learning about our stories, views, and experiences regarding civic engagement in higher education. I resonate with this type of conversational interview because it is similar to the one-to-one relational meetings I learned as an organizer. This type of two-way conversation is similar to what Miles Horton and Paulo Freire (1990) did in their spoken book *We Make the Road by Walking*. In the beginning of their conversation, Freire says to Horton that a spoken book "should give us a duality in the conversation, a certain relaxation, a result of losing seriousness in thinking while talking" (p. 5). During my conversational interviews, I tried to create this back-and-forth atmosphere of relaxation, while also discussing matters important to me and those I interviewed. In effect, we were participating in cocreating knowledge, which, in many cases, advanced our thinking about our work and about action-related strategies. That is, it advanced our civic agency. My hope is that those who read this book also engage with me and those whose voices you will read about, who have shared with me in this learning journey.

Community Organizing: My Birthright

I was born and raised in the state of Chihuahua, in northern Mexico. Although my parents met in Chihuahua, during the first few years of their marriage they lived in a hacienda in the state of Durango, where my father worked. My parents had 13 children; I was number 12, the second to the youngest. There were 11 women and 2 men. My father had about 3 years of schooling, and my mother probably only a single year. I am the only child who attended college. My younger brother entered high school but did not finish. Three of my sisters finished elementary school. The rest of my siblings had probably 1 to 3 years of schooling, in part because they had to work with my father in the agricultural fields to contribute to supporting the family. All of my siblings had children. I did not, partially by chance and partially by choice. When I was growing up, my father worked in agriculture and my mother raised us, but she also sold food and candies she made at the house. During my lifetime, we lived in rental homes until I was 19 or 20, when my factory salary contributed to buying a house for the family.

My first job was at a General Electric factory in Ciudad Juárez, when I was 17. I worked there for 5 years. At the time, I had decided that I did not want to finish middle school, mainly, I know now, because I was afraid our poverty conditions would prevent me from staying in school until gradua-tion. We also had just moved to Ciudad Juárez, and I was afraid of the big city. I had lived in small towns most of my life. My parents moved four times by the time I was 16, mostly looking for work. Within the first year of my job at the factory, noticing the harsh working conditions there, I decided to go back to school. Experiencing injustice at the factory—like not being allowed to use the bathroom or attend to a bleeding finger because this would slow production—made me want to study social work.

My community organizing practice began when I was a young, under-graduate student of social work at the *Universidad Autonoma de Ciudad Juárez* in the 1970s. During this time, a group of classmates and I realized that the school did not offer community organizing field placement and decided to create our ideal version of fieldwork, which resulted in a project to organize in rural communities in the *Valle de Juárez*. We distributed ourselves in vari-ous small towns lined up along the Mexico-U.S. border, all located within a 3-hour driving distance southeast of Ciudad Juárez. We organized on various issues, including education, water, and health care, for over a year. Through this experience my classmates and I began learning about community organ-izing but also about institutional organizing, as we navigated the university system to convince our professors and university authorities to make a vehi-cle and a driver available to transport 6 to 10 of us to the *Valle de Juárez*. Every Saturday and/or Sunday morning a university-owned bus dropped me and my classmates in the towns where we were organizing, and the same bus would return at the end of the day to take us back to Ciudad Juárez. This is how we, as students, used our evolving civic agency to create a new space that would address our educational interests. Navigating through the univer-sity's system itself turned out to be quite an educational experience, one that taught us a great deal about how to understand and leverage power within the institution. Thus began my life's work as a community organizer.

Defining *Community Organizing*

Throughout my professional life I have been part of a wide range of organizing approaches, including rural organizing in Mexico, neighborhood and resident based, short-term mobilization and protest, union, environmental, electoral, and broad-based organizing in the United States. Most people think of community organizing as activism, but there is an important distinction between the two.

Mark Rudd (2013) realized the importance of understanding this difference after hearing from many young people who believed that "nothing anyone does can ever make a difference." Intrigued by such a sense of powerlessness, Rudd decided to look into where this might originate. His conclusion is that young people are so removed from the experience of successful social change movements, such as those in the 1960s, that they seem to assume that these movements just happened, unaware of the political education, planning, and strategizing that were part of such movements. This is important because it helps explain why they feel defeated by recent unsuccessful antiwar protests. Rudd began to understand these young people's sense of powerlessness when he read *Letters From Young Activists: Today's Rebels Speak Out* (Berger, Boudin, & Farrow, 2005). In that book, Andy Cornell, addressing punk rock activism, defines *activism* and *organizing* as the following:

> Activists are individuals who dedicate their time and energy to various efforts they hope will contribute to social, political, or economic change. Organizers are activists who, in addition to their own participation, work to move other people to take action and help them develop skills, political analysis and confidence within the context of organizations. Organizing is a process—creating long-term campaigns that mobilize a certain constituency to press for specific demands from a particular target, using a defined strategy and escalating tactics. (pp. 72–73)

Rudd interprets Cornell's words, saying, "In other words, it's not enough for punks to continually express their contempt for mainstream values through their alternate identity; they've got to move toward 'organizing masses of people.' Aha! Activism = self-expression; organizing = movement-building" (pp. 72–73).

Activism thus defined is often expressed through anger and frustration about something considered an injustice. Activists are more likely to organize through mobilization and protest. These two activities can be effective when there is an urgency to block an action damaging a community, such as building a new prison without residents' input or in electoral campaigns. However, these are often short-term projects and are not always focused on building a collective of leadership involved in long-term societal and institutional culture transformation. The Occupy movement against economic inequality, which started in New York in September 2011, is an example of activism through massive mobilization. Although powerful, it dwindled almost as quickly as it had grown. In fact, much to my surprise, in a class on leadership in the community I taught at USC in the fall of 2012 none of the students (most of whom were students coming from low-income neighborhoods) had heard of it. Mobilization of this type, as the movement founders and activists found out, is hard to sustain for the long term.

Long-term, sustainable cultural and societal transformation, as Cornell's description establishes, is most successful when it includes a strategy for political education and leadership development (Berger et al., 2005). This type of education for successful movement building is also addressed by Horton and Freire (1990). The women's and the civil rights movements are examples of this type of long-term cultural and societal change. They both lasted a number of years; had a clear goal; and emphasized intentional, ongoing leadership training and development. The United Farm Workers Union is another such example, which, although it may not have the same level of power or visibility that it once had, continues to exist even after its founding leader, Cesar Chavez, died in 1993.

Given this confusion between activism and organizing, it is not surprising that organizing to create change in higher education might be perceived as mobilization and protest aimed at fighting those in positions of power, in this case senior administrators. In the community organizing approach I use in higher education, however, conversation, political education, deliberation, relationship building, and relational power are the foundation. This is something I took away from working with the IAF. I will explain more about the IAF, and about the organizing approach I use in academia, in chapter 2.

Organization of the Chapters

The premise of this book is that community organizing can help create a culture that values and rewards civically engaged scholarship, thus advancing higher education's public, democratic mission. I demonstrate how this takes place through lessons I have learned from experience and research in various institutions and in various contexts. I also discuss how the influence of dominant market forces has created antidemocratic conditions that make it difficult for civically engaged scholarship to be valued and rewarded, and consequently, this also makes it difficult to create reciprocal campus-community partnerships. I introduce these key themes in this chapter. I also emphasize the essential role of our personal narratives in creating change in higher education, give an introduction to the concept of community organizing, and share parts of my own narrative. In chapter 2, I elaborate in detail the specific community organizing approach I have been using in higher education for over a decade. In chapter 3, with voices from faculty, students, and community partners, I illustrate how this specific approach developed at Occidental College, where I first integrated community organizing with civic engagement. In chapter 4, I elaborate on the influence of the market in higher education through a discussion of neoliberalism. I make a connection between neoliberalism and the business models adapted by many colleges and universities, and how this affects the institutionalization of civically engaged scholarship. I end with a discussion of the concept of reciprocity as it pertains to creating reciprocal civic engagement partnerships. I illustrate these themes with excerpts from interviews at Maynooth University and at USC. In chapter 5, I summarize key themes of the book and make a strong argument for the use of community organizing practices to transform the culture of higher education and society in general. I emphasize the role of our personal stories and the intentional and strategic building of collective leadership. Most of all, this book is a narrative of my personal and professional journey of over a decade, and of how I have gone about cocreating spaces where democracy can be enacted and individual, institutional, and community transformation can occur.

2

FOUR COMMUNITY
ORGANIZING PRACTICES

Creating Culture Change

*B*road-based organizing "is a 'relational' and 'institutional' approach to
social change that relies on the local knowledge of ordinary citizens
to drive policy change and craft solutions to some of our most vexing
social problems" (Amos Institute of Public Life, 2017). As the term implies,
this type of organizing focuses on building a collective of different types
of institutions and groups (e.g., religious institutions, schools, unions, and
nonprofit organizations), representing a diversity of ethnicities and political
orientations. The type of organizing I have been practicing in higher education is broad based in the sense that it includes various stakeholders within
and outside of higher education institutions. The following is a story of my
work as an IAF broad-based organizer prior to working in higher education.

IAF Broad-Based Organizing

I first heard about the IAF while working in Albuquerque, New Mexico, on
environmental issues in 1990. At the time, I had lived in the United States
for eight years, but until I moved to Albuquerque I had not found opportunities to work as a community organizer. I had lived in Chicago for six years
and in Los Angeles for two years, and I had worked in two nonprofit organizations and one alternative high school for Latino adults. When I moved to
Albuquerque my main goal was to figure out once and for all whether I could
find a way to be a community organizer in the United States. In this search,
I found an environmental organization in Albuquerque and initially began
to work as a volunteer, helping it raise funds. I later became the director (and
only staff). One day, after about six months of doing this work I commented

to the pastor of the Catholic church that hosted the organization that I was feeling the need to further my organizing skills. He suggested we visit the IAF organization in El Paso, Texas, a four-hour drive south of Albuquerque. I called the lead organizer there, and she agreed to host both of us for a visit.

When we arrived, we were met by a group of around six experienced leaders from member churches and the local IAF organizer. One by one the leaders told us their stories and the reasons why they were part of the IAF. The organizer said very little. Then two leaders took us on a tour of the *colonias*, economically marginalized communities along the U.S.-Mexico border, where residents had bought undeveloped land with the promise that these areas would become fully urbanized. People built their homes and found themselves with unpaved streets, no water or electricity for years to come, and no access to government or politicians who would help them solve their problems. In essence, they had no access to power. These leaders told us that they had joined the IAF through their church, and that they had learned how to organize. They talked about meeting with politicians and giving them the same tour they gave us, and that they now had the skills and the power to improve their communities. This realization of their own power, they said, had come as a result of the IAF's trainings and their involvement in political actions around their communities.

When we returned to the IAF office, the leaders told us that they wanted to organize in New Mexico and asked if we could start this process. We agreed, and I attended the IAF's national 10-day training (currently weeklong) a few months after this visit, in Texas. The training included a statewide action, where leaders like the ones I had met in El Paso engaged in political discourse with Ann Richards, then governor of Texas, in an exchange of political power and asked her to commit staff and resources to work with them on specific issues in their respective regions. The governor agreed to all that she was asked to do. It was now up to the leaders to follow up to make her accountable. As trainees we were guests observing this action. Our goal was to experience what public discourse and political, democratic collective action look and feel like. I still feel emotional when I remember the electrically charged people-power felt in the room, where hundreds of IAF leaders from various cities in Texas cheered in support of their representatives onstage. I was also emotional when I heard immigrant leaders powerfully and assertively talk to the governor in Spanish, while a translator interpreted. After the action, we observed the evaluation, which was led by one of the IAF organizers. "How do you feel?" asked the organizer, and thus began the evaluation. He said that it was important to process feelings first, before analyzing what took place in the action. This was followed by recognition of the leaders who played specific roles on the stage and a teaching piece on what had been accomplished.

I rode the bus back to the hotel where the training was held, full of emotions. I knew then that I wanted to be an IAF organizer.

I went back to Albuquerque and began doing one-to-ones with religious leaders, and then got some of them together for a meeting where IAF organizer Ernesto Cortes spoke to them about creating an organization in the state. I helped get funding to hire the first organizer and I went back to Los Angeles. I joined the staff of the IAF organization in South Central Los Angeles in 1992, two months before the Rodney King trial was the catalyst of the civil unrest that April. During the following eight years, I worked in Los Angeles, in Sonoma and Napa Counties, and in the San Francisco Bay area in northern California.

Between 1990 and 2000, my primary job as an IAF organizer entailed recruiting community organizations and religious institutions of various denominations and finding leaders whom I trained and mentored. I also organized actions where these leaders played roles similar to what I saw in Texas when I attended 10-day training. One example of these actions took place in Santa Rosa, California, in the late 1990s. The action focused primarily on immigration-related issues, about which leaders engaged with an immigration official from San Francisco. Their main demand was that the process of applying for citizenship be streamlined.

Once a year I joined all organizers from the West Coast region on retreats where we shared our work, challenges, and new discoveries. We learned about the latest writings and strategies informing our organizing work. We read, wrote, and reflected on our work. We also used this time to check in with each other through one-to-one conversations. The IAF's national training curriculum is not widely publicized, in part because participating in the training is only by invitation. Invitation is usually done by IAF organizers, and those invited have demonstrated prior to the training that they are currently or intend to be involved in the local IAF organization. The IAF website states the following very general information for its curriculum:

> The curriculum includes how to: understand power; discover and act on the interests of your institution; identify and develop sustainable leadership; think and act strategically; and most important, how to engage in real conversations about the mission and democratic action of your institution—including the ability to discuss, argue, negotiate and compromise—while forming and maintaining collaborative relationships that ultimately lead to action. (Industrial Areas Foundation, 2017)

These practices are one-to-one meetings, creating a collective of leaders, analyzing power dynamics, and ongoing critical reflection.

During my tenure with IAF, I taught parts of the curriculum in Spanish several times, and the themes I taught included breaking problems into winnable issues, understanding power and power structures in society, building leadership, doing one-to-one meetings, and taking time for reflection. I drew the four organizing practices from this curriculum and have made adaptations according to context. These practices are one-to-one meetings, building a collective of leaders, understanding and using power, and ongoing critical reflection.

The Four Practices

In this section, I offer a detailed discussion of the four organizing practices I use in my civic engagement work.

Practice 1: One-to-One Meetings

The main purpose of one-to-one meetings is to build public relationships; therefore, their tone is conversational and based on a genuine interest to learn about things that really matter to those with whom we meet. This is called *self-interest*, and it usually comes out of aspects of people's personal stories, rather than factual, superficial conversations. Self-interest is about things that matter to people enough to move them to become involved in public life for the long term. Dick Harmond, a former West Coast organizer, refers to it as *soul-interest*, which helps remove the notion that this type of self-interest relates to being selfish and individualistic. A focus on finding out about people's self-interest is different from individual or group meetings that aim to convince people to join our cause, which may help encourage people to attend a meeting or participate in a training or a political action but is not likely to engage people in the long term.

> *The main purpose of one-to-one meetings is to build public relationships; therefore, their tone is conversational, based on a genuine interest to learn about things that really matter to those with whom we meet.*

Paul Osterman, an academic at Massachusetts Institute of Technology, studied the IAF network for several years. In *Gathering Power*, a book about the IAF, Osterman (2002) states that one-to-ones aim primarily to build relationships. Thus, these meetings are conversations around figuring out what really matters to leaders or potential leaders with whom we meet. Osterman describes one-to-ones in the following way:

The goal of these conversations is to identify people with the talent (even if yet unrealized and perhaps unrecognized) and motivation to engage in political activity. In searching for talent, the organizers typically avoid people who bring with them a preset activist agenda. These people, in the view of the organizers, too frequently act as gatekeepers. Rather, a good potential leader is someone who is "relational," that is, who has a wide network of contacts via a leadership role in a school, a church, a neighborhood club, and who has some anger that can be tapped into and channeled into those with whom we meet. (pp. 44–45)

Another way in which organizers look for leaders or potential leaders takes place through small group meetings, which the IAF calls *house meetings*. Both individual and group meetings are based on learning about each other's stories, in search for identifying things that have meaning, that really matter to participants of these meetings. Osterman (2002) cites a priest from a large church who is a leader in an IAF organization in the Rio Grande Valley, in Texas. This priest speaks about the importance of story in house meetings, which also relates to the role of story in individual meetings. The priest gives examples of how to have meaningful conversations that aim at learning through our stories:

You ask where is meaning and significance in your story? What brings meaning to your life? Who are the models? Who are the people who touch you? Who inspires you? What are the significant things that have happened in your life? . . . Those stories are used so that you can connect and listen to other people so that we begin to listen to many people and realize that we're in the same boat. We're experiencing the same frustration. So we begin to share the pain and make the pain public. (p. 47)

Making the pain public involves taking action that includes researching specific issues that emerge from these conversations, and finding out who has the power and resources to create change around such issues.

Following, I discuss some of the key aspects of these relational one-to-one meetings.

Public, Not Private Relationships
Because organizing for democratic engagement is political, it is important to distinguish between private and public relationships. One way to think about this distinction is that private relationships (which I think of as relationships with relatives, and with possibly a few very close friends) tend to be glued by unconditional love and kinship, whereas public relationships are based on respect and accountability. This distinction is not divided by a hard, thick

line, but rather by a very porous, fluid line through which boundaries can be and are often crossed. Yet if we do not make this distinction clear we run the risk of confusing public spaces, such as our higher education institutions, organizations, places where we work, and even places of worship, with private spaces, such as our homes. When this happens, feelings of friendship, love, and loyalty can make it difficult to hold people in positions of power accountable. An example of the comments from a student in a Leadership in the Community class I taught at USC can help clarify this point. This student's community-based project, part of my CBL class, was organizing for gender-neutral facilities on campus. She and a group of students met with administrators who had the power and resources to create change around this issue. Following the meeting, she commented that she was disappointed that though administrators had told the students that they were part of the campus family, administrators were uninterested in talking to students about requests related to student well-being. She felt that public statements about students being part of a big, institutional family were not real, and that she was considered family only as a marketing strategy. This was an important teaching opportunity, and discussing the difference between public and private relationships in class helped her realize that school is part of the public and not the private sphere. This kind of situation is much more common than most of us realize, regardless of the type of institutions we happen to be part of. Because this is such an important aspect of organizing and of building public life skills, it was a common theme in IAF meetings to plan and to evaluate actions, such as the one I first witnessed in Texas. For example, in IAF actions, leaders in a position that involves interacting with a public official onstage role-play prior to the action how they are to act if the elected official approaches this leader for a hug or a kiss on the check (acts that, in this political arena, are considered to be in the realm of private relationships). Allowing for these types of private gestures can be confusing especially if these leaders have not experienced interacting with people in power in this way. Thus, such leaders often have to practice countering these private acts with a firm handshake.

Probing and Agitation
When trying to learn about what really matters to people, probing helps. Probing can be done by asking questions like "What does your work mean to you" rather than questions like "How do you like your work?" Or put in a different way, the "why" is more important than the "what." It is important to distinguish probing from prying, in that probing is done with an awareness of boundaries set by those with whom we meet. While probing, *agitation* can be helpful. The purpose of agitation in a one-to-one meeting is to challenge complacency, or a sense that things cannot be changed by people

who are not part of the predominant power structure. However, we need to distinguish between agitation and aggravation. The purpose of agitation is not to say things to aggravate people, and it is important to sense how much we can agitate based on the level of trust between the two people in the meeting. In my experience, one of the most effective ways to agitate those with whom we meet and, in the process, ourselves takes place when we exchange our personal stories. In a genuinely engaged conversation when we talk about things that make us tick or that hurt or who our heroes and heroines are, we stir up each other's emotions and give each other inspiration, energy, and hope to take collective action we may not have felt capable of doing before. Agitation can also help us understand the world as it is, unjust as it may be, so that we can then figure out how to create the world as we would like it to be. Probing and agitation are the opposite of having a meeting that stays at the superficial, factual level, with no possibilities for building a public relationship and with no organizing consequences.

Suspending Judgment

Another important element of building public relationships is to try to suspend judgment of the people with whom we are meeting, even if they are sharing information with which we highly agree or disagree. If the other people sense we are being judgmental we will lose their trust, and the conversation will not lead to relationship building. Nor is it useful to be analyzing or anticipating what answers or responses we may get, as this will only prevent us from being present and genuinely engaged in the conversation.

Selectively Finding Leaders

In finding others to cocreate and take collective action it is important to be selective. While one-to-one meetings can help us find others who can colead with us, thus also cothinking and costrategizing for action, not everyone we meet with will turn into coleaders, for all kinds of reasons. Perhaps they are not interested in being part of the collective we are trying to build, or they are not clear about their politicalness or their civic agency, for example. Therefore, in order to find enough leaders to join us we must do as many one-to-one meetings as possible, on an ongoing basis. In my experience of teaching workshops on how to do these meetings one of the biggest barriers in finding leaders is that we do not do enough one-to-one meetings, and the main reason for this is that we do not think we know how to do them right, or we think we need to learn all there is to know about one-to-ones before starting. The truth I have experienced is that there is no right or wrong way to do these meetings. If we want to be more skilled in this practice, we simply must do them regularly. I realize, however, that another major barrier is that our culture does not value or even understand the point of being relational. Our culture values quick results and constant hyperactivity, neither of which leads to building public relationships. Therefore, building the discipline of doing one-to-ones requires us to schedule them the same way we schedule the rest of our work and, if possible, integrate them into our regular routines.

Mentoring/Coaching/Guiding

Once we find leaders or potential leaders we need to invest in their development so that they learn the specific skills and practices necessary to be publically engaged with us and others in the leadership collective. This can include taking them to meetings with us where we think they can learn about what we are organizing about; assigning them specific tasks that are appropriate for their level of leadership skill, interest, and commitment; and including them in group workshops on leadership and organizing skills.

Following are important elements to keep in mind when planning one-to-one meetings:

- Getting names from others we know and trust, and whose names we can use to credential ourselves when calling/e-mailing. For instance, if we are looking for faculty who are civically engaged, we can find them by talking to one faculty member, one student, or one administrator we know and trust and who can give us names of one or more civically engaged faculty members and so on.
- Looking for people who are well regarded and who are skilled at building relationships, on campus and/or in the community, depending on whom we are trying to meet.
- Looking for diversity of ethnicity, gender, political views, discipline, and so forth as well as diversity of stakeholders and sectors in society, as opposed to looking only for the "usual" suspects, or only those with whom we are comfortable.
- Introducing ourselves by briefly stating who we are and why we want to meet with them.
- Stating clearly what dates/times we are proposing to meet; telling those we are meeting how long the meeting will take (e.g., 30–45 minutes); and sticking to it, as this can build or break trust.

After the meeting, it is good to take brief notes on what we learned about their self-interest, their leadership potential, parts of their story, and whether we might want to have a follow-up meeting and/or invite them to a leadership meeting or training.

Practice 2: Building a Collective of Leaders

Building a long-term collective of leaders is essential in growing a movement, and it is a process of building the necessary knowledge and resources for our public engagement work. This point usually comes after a series of one-to-one meetings. There is a great deal of talk about leadership in higher education, government, the civic sector, and the business sector. However, many contemporary leadership theorists, such as Nohria and Khurana (2010) and Ospina and Foldy (2010), concur that we are lacking clear concepts of leadership that are helpful for our current organizational and social dilemmas. These theorists believe the main reasons why we are stuck in our theory and practice of leadership to be that we are still trying to resolve the question of whether leaders are born or if they can be trained, and that we still operate based on the image of a single, smart, articulate, and charismatic leader and his or her followers. There is, for instance, a misconception that leaders such as Martin Luther King Jr., Rosa Parks, Dolores Huerta, and Cesar Chavez were somehow chosen and especially gifted, and that they became leaders overnight. In reality, these leaders benefited from community and political organizing training prior to becoming famous in their respective organizing movements. Parks and many other civil rights leaders, for instance, were trained at the Highlander Folk School in Tennessee (Horton & Freire, 1990), and Chavez and Huerta were trained at the IAF organization Community Service Organizations in California (Texas Archival Resources Online, n.d.).

> *Building a long-term collective of leaders is essential in growing a movement, and it is a process of building the necessary knowledge and resources for our public engagement work.*

Understanding that exemplary leaders are not born with a special gift to be leaders but are people like many of us—who have a desire to create a better, more just world and who decide to respond to the call, invest in their leadership development, and find others to join them—can serve to encourage more of us to step forward. In the same CBL class at USC mentioned earlier, one of the most rewarding moments for me was when toward the end of the semester, students shifted from simply being inspired by exemplary leaders to recognizing that they themselves can be and in many cases already are leaders.

Fortunately, this realization about the state of our leadership practices is pushing us to come up with models of leadership that can be more responsive to our current organizational and societal dilemmas. These models of leadership also offer more relational and interactive processes between leaders and followers. Thus, for instance, Ospina and Foldy (2010) argue in an article based on a study of social change organizations that in a relational approach leadership is distributive among many, rather than concentrating on a single leader.

Following are some of the qualities in leaders or potential leaders I look for through research interviews and through classes and workshops I teach:

- An understanding of their personal narrative, who they are, and where they come from
- A vision of the world as it should be, while understanding the world as it is and realizing the importance of working within it
- An understanding of the role of power in organizing to create the world as it should be
- A willingness to learn, act, and reflect together
- A commitment to being accountable to oneself and to others with whom we organize, and to making others in the team accountable
- The ability to work with tension and uncertainty, and to see failure as a learning opportunity
- The ability to celebrate, laugh, and have fun in the process

These qualities are ideal, of course. Therefore, we need to use our best judgment in deciding who is or has potential to be a leader in the future. Then we need to look for opportunities for these people to get involved in our work, test whether our judgment was right, and continue working on our own leadership development as a journey.

Practice 3: Understanding and Using Power

> The moment the word *power* is mentioned it is as though hell had been opened, exuding the stench of the devil's cesspool of corruption. It evokes images of cruelty, dishonesty, selfishness, arrogance, dictatorship, and abject suffering. (Alinsky, 1971, p. 51)

Saul D. Alinsky, the founder of the IAF, was known for using direct, often harsh language as a way to agitate and to avoid confusion about what is really needed to create long-lasting societal change. He refers to Lord Acton's famous phrase "Power tends to corrupt, and absolute power corrupts absolutely" as a phrase that often gets misquoted as "Power corrupts, and absolute power corrupts absolutely" (Alinsky, 1971). This leaves out "tends to," which for Alinsky has implications for the meaning we give to the word, and thus for our discomfort with it (Alinsky, 1971). In contrast to this general perception of power, Michael Gecan, a senior IAF organizer, claims that in order to move from the world as it is—based on market, material values—to the world as it should be—based on human rights and values—we need to understand and exercise power. That is, power is an essential ingredient in organizing to create the world as we would like it to be (Gecan, 2002). Ernesto Cortes, another senior IAF organizer, defines *power* as "nothing more than the ability to act in your own behalf, to act for your own interest" (Rogers, 1990, p. 31). In reaction to comments from leaders about power's potential to be corruptive, at an evaluation of an action where they had invited former San Antonio mayor Henry Cisneros, Cortes replied, "Just as we know that power tends to corrupt, we also know that powerlessness corrupts. We've got a lot of people who've never developed an understanding of power. They've been institutionally trained to be passive" (Rogers, 1990, p. 31).

Many stakeholders in civic engagement have also been institutionally trained to be passive, suspicious of those in power, and uncomfortable with using power on their own behalf. This is true at all levels, depending on what role we play in our institutions and in society. For instance, through my civic engagement work since 2001, and in all institutions that I have been part of, I have seen community partners and students defer to faculty as the ones who know and have power, and I also have seen faculty defer to administrators and administrators to board of trustees members and funders. In his chapter "Relational Theory and the Discourses of Power" Kenneth J. Gergen (1995) argued that *power* has been defined and used by predominant politics or worldviews in ways that are divisive, using examples such as powerful versus powerless, rich versus poor, conservatives versus progressives, and so on, and that this worldview affects the way we act and the actions we take to create change. Thus, for example, he stated that hierarchical models of authority and the internal worlds within sectors of society are products of the predominant worldview.

Discussions about power are essential for organizing purposes, but they are also difficult for many of us, in part because we have a sort of love/hate affair with power in general, depending on which side of the equation of power we happen to be. *Empowerment,* a term familiar to many in the education and public sectors, is usually related to individual self-confidence, and it is different from power in a political context. Meredith Minkler and Nina Wallerstein (2011) distinguish between this and a broader, more political definition, which views *empowerment* "as a social action process by which individuals, communities, and organizations gain mastery over their lives in the context of changing their social and political environments to improve equity and quality of life" (p. 34, citing Rappaport, 1984, and Wallerstein, 1992).

Too, we often think of power and love as opposites. In a speech to the Southern Christian Leadership Conference in Atlanta on August 16, 1967, Martin Luther King Jr. gave this definition of *power*: "Power properly understood is nothing but the ability to achieve purpose. It is the strength required to bring about social, political, and economic change." King then addressed the confusion that exists about the difference between power and love:

> One of the great problems of history is that the concepts of love and power have usually been contrasted as opposites, polar opposites, so that love is identified with a resignation of power, and power with a denial of love. . . . Now, we got to get this thing right. What is needed is a realization that power without love is reckless and abusive, and that love without power is sentimental and anemic. . . . Power at its best is love . . . implementing the demands of justice, and justice at its best is love correcting everything that stands against love. (King, 1967)

To counter this image of power as a negative concept, the IAF distinguishes between power-over and power-with, defining *power-with* as relational, rather than one-sided, top-down power. With this definition of power, it is then our responsibility to understand it and use it, and it is an essential part of our political education and of our civic agency. That is, we need to be specific, intentional, and aware of our own power and that of others, conceptually and in practice, and we need to be clear about how we define *power*.

One way we operationalize power is by analyzing who has the power to block or facilitate our organizing efforts. That is, we analyze power to examine and understand the web of relationships we need to build, as well as to understand challenges and opportunities for our engagement work. At IA summer organizing institutes in 2013 and 2014, participants worked in teams organized by institutions and communities where they work and engaged in analyzing power dynamics in the context of civic engagement. Through reflection and discussion, in some cases accompanied by drawing with markers and butcher paper, their power analysis helped them assess who has power and resources to block or facilitate their work. This understanding of institutional power dynamics helped them begin to think about strategies to advance their work, which led them to think of specific people whom they needed to reach out to for one-to-one meetings on their campuses and in their communities. This type of analysis leads to realistic and focused strategies, and it can be more effective than going about our work as a daily routine, without a pragmatic and realistic understanding of whether our work will advance the overall purpose of civic engagement on our campus.

One way we operationalize power is by analyzing who has the power to either block or facilitate our organizing efforts. That is, we analyze power to examine and understand the web of relationships we need to build, as well as to understand challenges and opportunities for our engagement work.

Practice 4: Ongoing Critical Reflection

I first heard about the concept of reflecting regularly about work and about life in general in the 10-day IAF national training I attended in Texas, mentioned earlier. In the last day, after covering all the basics of broad-based organizing, we closed the training with a three-hour session on the importance of integrating reflection, spending time with our loved ones, and taking personal time off, on our weekly planners. As an organizer, I was required to write reflective reports at least once a month, but I have to say that at first I did not see the point. With time, reflecting regularly became an activity I looked forward to, especially after I noticed that when I skipped reflection my work and often my personal life suffered. Adult education theorist Jack Mezirow (1990) affirms that reflection enables us to correct distortions in our beliefs and that it improves our problem-solving ability. He adds that "critical reflection involves a critique of the presuppositions on which our beliefs have been built" (p. 1). Brazilian educator Paulo Freire (1995) taught agricultural workers how to read and write by reflecting about their historical reality of oppression as a way to develop their power to understand and transform their reality. The way one IAF senior organizer put it is that reflection is to the mind what digestion is to the body, and that it is not good for us to be walking around with a bunch of undigested thoughts and ideas. The result of practicing reflection regularly during the years I worked with the IAF is that I now integrate this practice in everything I do. I have done this with staff I have supervised and with students in classes I teach by having them write short reflective papers and then discussing them in meetings or classes. I also integrate reflection in workshops I facilitate and in my civic engagement work in general. For the sake of organizing and our public engagement work, reflection is essential in at least four areas:

1. Evaluation: In order to deepen our learning, and with it our work, short debriefing evaluations after meetings and events can help us assess if we met our goals, and how we can do this better in the future. This also helps debrief how people are feeling about the meeting or event, rather than leaving with unprocessed, undigested feelings that may cause them not to come back or not to participate as much, feeling unrecognized or confused.

2. Power check: Through reflection we update ourselves on the evolving nature of power dynamics within our institutions and communities, and in society in general. Civic engagement is deeply political, and political dynamics are constantly shifting. Updating our power analysis can then inform our decisions about whether we need to make changes in our strategies, approach new people for one-to-ones so we can find new coleaders, or revisit allies to check if they are still supportive of our work.

3. Accountability: Reflecting about our goals and responsibilities is not just about reporting on projects. Rather, it is about accountability on what we committed to do individually and as a collective. As mentioned earlier, being able to make each other accountable is a major aspect of being in public and not private relationships. It is a way of respecting our work and each other, and of advancing our goals. Giving reasons and justifications for why we did not fulfill our commitments to ourselves and seeking to be excused or forgiven do not advance our goals, as important as those reasons may be. Discussing whether our previous commitments are still doable, reassessing ways to fulfill our commitments in the future, and even asking for help from others, on the other hand, are all ways of being accountable.

4. Self-interest check: Reflection also gives us an opportunity to revisit our individual self-interest, and its alignment with our leadership collective's and institution's vision for change. In some cases, this is related to our personal narratives and our reasons for wanting to create change through our engagement work. To me, self-interest is similar to soul-interest, and therefore I view individual and collective reflection as an opportunity to nourish our souls.

Integrating Organizing in Civic Engagement

To summarize this chapter, I propose that in order to create culture change in higher education through community organizing we must do one-to-one meetings, build a collective of leadership, understand the role of power in our civic engagement work, and reflect about our progress on an ongoing basis (Figure 2.1). The following are some elements that can help us integrate and sustain community organizing in our civic engagement work:

- Work strategically and selectively. This includes deciding where to focus our time and energy, planning for meetings ahead of time, and having a clear purpose for meetings we hold or attend.
- Rotate who facilitates meetings we hold, and delegate responsibilities as a way to create learning opportunities for others.
- Build and sustain relationships with key stakeholders.
- Create and abide by clear accountability standards, which ideally are created by the leadership collective.
- Understand and know how to use relational power.
- Identify issues to work on based on our interest combined with the interest(s) of the people with whom we are working.
- Treat issues as tools to develop leadership and to expand support for the larger vision of our engagement work, not as the ultimate goals.
- Create opportunities for learning, acting, and reflecting together.

Figure 2.1. Summarizing the four community organizing practices.

Creating and sustaining these elements may seem daunting, but it is important to understand and embrace the value of process and the incremental aspect of this type of work. The state of our democratic society is reflected in our campuses, organizations, and communities, where decisions are constantly being made unilaterally or by a small group of people in positions of power, and these decisions are imposed upon the majority. Institutions that foster democracy are continuously shrinking in all sectors. Similarly, Harry Boyte (2009) comments that "institutions of many kinds—from schools to nonprofits, businesses to congregations, government agencies to universities—have lost community roots" (p. 2). As a result, "institutions have come to be conceived as abstract, bureaucratic, and largely impervious to culture change, defined by rules, regulations, structures, and procedures, not as human creations that can in turn be re-created" (p. 2). Therefore, it is important to create and sustain spaces where the work of democracy can be fostered, and where citizens can take collective action as cocreators of such spaces, thus acting on their individual and collective civic agency. This is what organizing is about. There are many examples where faculty, students, and community partners are organizing such democratic spaces. I present one such example, through the work that took place at Occidental's CCBL, in chapter 3.

3

HOW COMMUNITY
ORGANIZING EVOLVED AT
OCCIDENTAL COLLEGE

I think that my practice as a professional was changed by what we were doing. . . . I think it's the relational thing . . . and the organizing lens. You know, I'll say, "Oh, we need to do a power analysis," so we will do a power analysis. . . . When I'm thinking about wanting to make some changes here at this school, I'm going to look at my faculty, I'm going to look at who my people are, I'm going to look at where everybody is and I think about my leverage points . . . or my tipping points. But I'm going to go about that very much in an organizing way. I'm going to have one-to-one conversations with people; I'm going to try to find out what their interests are. I'm going to try to find out if I can put people together around an interest and I can create something meaningful for them, so they can work forward from that place. (Katherine Harrison, public school educator and former CCBL community partner, personal communication, October 10, 2015)

E arly in the fall semester of 2001, I was preparing for an interview for what would become my job as director of the CCBL at Occidental College in Los Angeles. I was full of apprehension. I did not want to apply for the job, but Peter Dreier, a politics professor whom I had met in the 1990s when I was a community organizer in South Central Los Angeles, insisted that I should apply. The CCBL had been created by a group of faculty working with then-president Ted Mitchell the summer of 2001. To me, the job description seemed too service oriented and not at all appealing, given my interest in creating societal change. My community organizing colleagues and friends, however, advised me to try to use my organizing background and skills and integrate this into my job description. They helped me see that I could explore this new opportunity to create societal change from a different angle. Although I was not entirely sure what this would look like on the ground, their advice was appealing. Thinking as an organizer, I decided to use the interview to find out about the visions and hopes for the CCBL, from all who were part of the interview. There were about a dozen people in the room including faculty, staff/administrators, one community partner, and one student. After hearing their visions about the center, it seemed to me that they too were interested in creating societal change.

Specifically, the answers I heard from faculty members led me to understand that some of them were already engaged with various Los Angeles communities. It sounded as if their work was political, passionate, and yet academic. They were what Harry Boyte (2013) calls *civic professionals* and involved in what Scott J. Peters (2010) describes as higher education's public purposes, work, and roles in a democratic society. In the words of Clare Snyder-Hall (2013), it seemed to me that "their work ha[d] meaning and that they [could] make a positive difference in the world" (p. 2). This gave me hope. I was no longer apprehensive. I was intrigued by their hopes and aspirations for the work of the center in supporting their civically engaged scholarship, and in making information and resources available to other faculty on the campus, across disciplines. I also learned that they were interested in changing the institutional culture in which civic engagement was viewed as charity and service to a culture that realized that this type of scholarship can be academically rigorous. In this chapter, I offer a picture of how we succeeded in creating this culture shift, and I illustrate this process through voices from various stakeholders.

Why Occidental

I took the job in the fall of 2001 and thus began a collective project with faculty, administration, students, and community partners to create the work of the center, which would survive several presidential transitions and my own tenure at Occidental. These stakeholders were involved as cocreators of the charge of the CCBL, and therefore this charge became part of their professional self-interest; in many cases, it transformed their professional practice. Katherine Harrison, quoted at the beginning of this chapter, was one of these cocreators of the work of the center. She was an important member and leader of the Northeast Education Strategies Group (NESG), which I discuss later.

Occidental is private, residential, small, undergraduate, and liberal arts focused, with a reputation for being politically progressive. The college is located 15 minutes northeast of downtown Los Angeles, nestled within a mix of low- and middle-income neighborhoods, thus offering a wide range of opportunities for faculty and students to engage with the community. Mitchell's education philosophy, which was inspired by John Dewey's experiential vision of urban education, was important in his interest in creating the CCBL. All these factors gave the CCBL a good chance to succeed.

The CCBL was housed in the president's office for the first few years. Prior to the CCBL was the Center for Volunteerism and Community. Mitchell and some faculty members felt that this center had contributed to creating a culture in which community-engaged pedagogies were treated as service and were not taken seriously academically by most faculty. The CCBL was funded mostly by the president's unrestricted funds until it became institutionalized in the Office of Academic Affairs in 2004, when a new dean of the college and vice president of academic affairs was hired. This moved the CCBL to the institutional budget. We viewed this transition as a sign that the CCBL was there for the long term, and that its focus was on curriculum-based community partnerships.

Integrating Community Organizing and Civic Engagement on the Ground

I approached my work at Occidental from a set of assumptions, which included the following:

- Treat the college as a community in and of itself.
- All communities have existing and/or potential leaders, and my job was to find them.
- Long-term transformational and reciprocal engagement must be cocreated and coassessed by relevant stakeholders from the college community and from communities outside of the college.
- Engagement should aim at transforming the college, partnering community organizations, and the community at large.

These assumptions emerged in response to what I learned about the field of civic engagement nationally, during my early years at Occidental, discussed in chapter 1. What I learned can be summed up in three concerns. First, many in the field of civic engagement were disappointed that the movement, begun in the 1980s, to increase intentional engagement between universities and communities had not yet led to transforming students and faculty into active, civically engaged citizens. Second, these pioneering scholars were concerned that academic institutions were not engaging with their surrounding communities based on reciprocity of interests, resources, and knowledge (Ehrlich, 2000; Maurrasse, 2001). Third, faculty interested in connecting their teaching and research to community projects discovered that their institutions not only did not reward this type of scholarship but also often penalized faculty for pursuing it. While organizations like Campus Compact were gaining traction by successfully rallying a number of higher education campuses to integrate civic engagement–related language into their mission statements, these moves were not always coupled with changes in institutional decisions and policies on tenure and promotion or on the adequate allocation of resources for civic engagement work. These three concerns were at the heart of the culture of higher education that required transformation in the early 2000s, and I would argue they are still relevant today, over a decade later. The aim of changing these aspects of academic culture is what underpinned my community organizing work at Occidental.

As I describe later in this chapter, the collective of cocreators and I used community organizing and were able to institutionalize community-based learning (CBL) and community-based research (CBR) across many departments and disciplines. We were also able to create a culture that acknowledges this way of teaching and research as civically engaged scholarship and that values the concept and the practice of reciprocal, mutually beneficial campus-community partnerships.

How Organizing Evolved

In this section I offer a detailed account of how the four organizing practices I described in chapter 2 evolved at Occidental. I illustrate this with stories and direct accounts from faculty, students, administrators, and community partners. I organize this section into the four organizing practices.

Practice 1: One-to-One Meetings

Within the first year of my work at Occidental I had more than 100 one-to-one meetings with administrators, faculty, students, and community partners. Because of the focus on creating a culture where civic engagement, specifically CBL and CBR, would be institutionally valued and rewarded, I focused at first on meeting with faculty, starting with faculty members who led the process of creating the CCBL and hiring its first director. Through these meetings, I learned about their views and experience regarding CBL and CBR and, in some cases, about the connection between their jobs and their personal stories—their self-interest. Many of these faculty members had worked at Occidental for a long time, and they spoke about their work with a sense of ownership for and commitment to the institution and the education it offered its students.

Politics professor Regina Freer is an example of this type of institutional commitment, and she resembles Wolin's (1989) description of politicalness mentioned in chapter 1. She was one of the founders of the CCBL and a member of the committee that had interviewed me, and she also became a cothinker and costrategist with me as this approach to civic engagement evolved.

Freer was actively involved in issues affecting low-income communities in Los Angeles prior to joining Occidental in 1996, and this work influenced her interest in creating a center that would offer guidance and resources for faculty and students interested in community engagement. To understand Freer's politicalness, it is important to know her story. Part of this story was featured in *Occidental Magazine* in the summer of 2012 (Borja, 2012):

> Born a year after the 1965 Watts riots—her mother is black, her father, white—she grew up in a South L.A. neighborhood whose ethnic footprint was gradually changing. After a racist landlord refused to rent a house to Freer's parents, the Freers bought another house down the block.

Her story has fueled her work as an activist, also leading to her appointment to serve on the Los Angeles Planning Commission in 2005, at the request of Mayor Antonio Villaraigosa. Her story has also informed her work as a civically engaged scholar. Freer's views on CBL included a clear vision for creating aspects of class syllabi and projects together with her community partners and with their interest, knowledge, and resources in mind. This vision proved to be crucial in our success in creating a culture where reciprocal engagement became a central concept and practice. Freer said, "Civic engagement is not charity. It's about partnership. We enter into a partnership not just to get, but to give. It's both" (Borja, 2012). While Freer was not yet tenured when I first came to Occidental, she already enjoyed the respect of her faculty colleagues, of students, and of senior administrators. Having credibility in the institution is an essential leadership quality, and this helped credential me as I approached others on the campus. In other words, when I approached others on campus with a request to meet with me, knowing that Freer was involved in the creation of the CCBL made it more likely that they would agree to meet. She was also able to help me understand the politics of the campus. Freer was one of the first faculty members to implement a CBL class that was intentionally based on shared interests and resources. Based on a long-term relationship Freer had with the staff at the Southern California Library, a nonprofit archival library in South Central Los Angeles, she approached the staff to explore the possibility of teaching a class on archival research for Occidental students at the library. The library staff members were interested,

> and through a series of meetings facilitated by the CCBL, the curriculum for a course was developed that would take students to the library, teach them archival methodology, have them produce finding aids for unprocessed archival collections, and then give community presentations to encourage young people in South LA to explore and use the collection. The class syllabus represented a negotiation of Dr. Freer's and the library's varied and shared interests. (Castillo, Freer, Guillen, & Maeda, 2015, p. 290)

I remember this class vividly, especially because Freer made arrangements to actually drive the students to the library every week, where she taught the class. We learned a great deal from this experience, as we together continued to guide other faculty on campus to design CBL classes. Freer commented on some of the lessons she learned, saying,

> Constant communication was critical for making midstream adjustments. . . . For example, I had to adjust my expectations of the amount of time the staff could devote to guiding the students, while the library staff had to adjust their expectations of the level of historical knowledge the students brought. (Castillo et al., 2015, pp. 290–291)

As we continued building a campus-wide movement to integrate reciprocal CBL throughout the campus, senior administrators and faculty with whom I was meeting gave me names of, and in some cases introduced me to, off-campus community leaders. One of the administrators introduced me briefly to Ref Rodriguez in 2002, who at the time was in the early stages of cofounding Partnerships to Uplift Communities (PUC), an organization of charter schools in northeast Los Angeles and in east San Fernando Valley. I followed up this brief introduction with a one-to-one meeting in Rodriguez's office, at the California Academy of Liberal Studies, a middle school, and one of the first of the now 16 PUC charter schools. In this meeting, Rodriguez shared that he was born and raised in northeast Los Angeles, that his family was originally from Mexico, and that he was passionate about access and equity for immigrant communities. He said he had decided to create good quality educational opportunities for children of his community, many of whom came from recent immigrant, Latino families.

A few months later I e-mailed Rodriguez; Juan Flecha, the principal of Eagle Rock High School; Freer; and Dick Cone, asking if they would be interested in meeting as a group to discuss what was emerging as common interests in access and equity through education. They all said they were interested, and in this meeting we began a relational, group process through which the NESG was born. This group later grew to include over a dozen school and community organization leaders, as well as Occidental faculty, administrators, students, and alumni. I elaborate on this group later in this chapter. To illustrate one-to-one meetings, I share excerpts from an interview I did with Rodriguez in the summer of 2012 as part of research for this book (in 2015, Rodriguez ran for Los Angeles School Board member, District 5 and won). In the following, Rodriguez offers a very detailed description of the feel as well as the purpose of one-to-one meetings, while remembering the meeting he and I had in his office in 2002:

> Rodriguez: I remember very succinctly the time, the day that you and I met in my office. . . . You were relatively new in your position . . . but I remember intuitively that the conversation felt different from the way that I had had conversations in the past or even moving forward with other folks that were potentially going to become partners. In fact, I remember distinctly that that wasn't even part of the conversation at the front end. There wasn't an ask. "This is what we're doing at the Center for Community-Based Learning and what would you be interested in?" It wasn't that. It was really getting to know me, my story, and a lot of listening. But that left a big impression on me. And I remember thinking, "I'd like to learn how to do that." . . . Of course, I'm talking about the relational one-to-ones, right?

> Avila: What did it do for you?

> Rodriguez: So, two things. One . . . it prompted me to be reflective. So the questions were not only about what we were doing as an institution, but it was a lot of the why. So getting to know me. Which in turn kind of led to, "Why the institution? Why [create] my middle school?" And so, it forced me to reflect and think about things that I had not thought about, or things that go on without being said. I take a lot of action and there's very little time to reflect as to why I'm taking those actions. And it was one of those first times where I had felt, "Oh . . . someone's interested in learning about why I started this. Where does it come from and what am I really trying to do and for what reason." So the questions . . . forced me to think with a different part of my brain. It wasn't the elevator pitch I could have given you about my institution, what we're trying to do. The [second] thing about it was that, in turn, I also got to know you a little bit. And in fact I remember thinking after you left, "I may never hear from her again because we didn't get to the business, but even if I don't, I feel like I know her a little bit and . . . I might reach out to her just for a whole other reason," but it wasn't like . . . there wasn't . . . sort of the next steps. And that left a big impression in just the way that I started to think about relationships in general. So that's a really key moment for me.

Rodriguez learned through our work together for several years after this first conversation that we did get to "the business" of this meeting. This business was in fact the exploration of a relationship, figuring out if our respective self-interests matched in a way that could lead to a long-term partnership, which would connect our self-interests with the interests of the collectives with which we each worked: PUC, Occidental, and the surrounding communities. It all began with a relational conversation about our mutual interests, as opposed to a meeting to try to convince him to partner with the CCBL.

Practice 2: Building a Collective of Leaders

Finding leaders who can stay involved in organizing and civic engagement for the long term is a relational, slow process, and it takes time. This is how, through one-to-one meetings, I found those who would be part of a collective of leaders in the CCBL's faculty committee, and later community partners who would be part of the NESG. The CCBL faculty committee came from costrategizing with Freer and others, and this led to a unanimous vote by the faculty assembly in favor of formalizing the committee in the spring of 2003. In other words, this faculty committee was part of faculty governance, thus deepening the integration of the CCBL into the campus. This proved to be of great help in our efforts to shift the image of CBL from service and volunteerism to an academically rigorous pedagogy. This new relationship with faculty informed specific programmatic activities of the CCBL. One such activity, which emerged from our understanding that faculty were receptive to CBL but many did not know how to go about it, was an annual summer CBL workshop, and later CBL/CBR workshop, which continued to take place after I left Occidental.

One-to-ones also helped me find leaders in the community; thus, the NESG was formed. (See chapter 2 for a description of desirable qualities in a leader.) As illustrated by Rodriguez, this relational process included learning about each other's stories in connection to our roles as educators, learning about community organizing practices, and negotiating with those in power on and off campus on education-related issues. One of the key NESG leaders was Celestina Castillo. After five years as a community partner she joined the CCBL staff as assistant director, and as of January 2017, she is the director of the center. While I met Freer and Rodriguez through my CCBL work, I met Castillo as a student in a community organizing class I taught at Los Angeles Trade-Tech College in 2000. I recognized her leadership potential then, and I reached out to her to explore her interest in becoming part of the campus-community leadership collective I was hoping to create. At the time, Castillo was working with a nonprofit organization. Following she describes her story as a multigeneration resident of one of Occidental's surrounding communities and her own leadership development, as well as the type of ongoing training that was part of building community and campus leadership.

> I am from Highland Park, one of the communities that surround the college, and a Latino neighborhood with low- to middle-income levels and a history of high dropout rates and poor-performing schools. My family has been in Highland Park for four generations. My maternal grandmother was from the Tohono O'odham Indian Reservation in southern Arizona. She came to Los Angeles in the late 1930s to find work after her mother and other family members had died. My grandfather was a Mexican American migrant farm worker from California who eventually settled in Los Angeles. In the late 1950s, my grandparents were the first nonwhite family to buy a home on our block. When they moved in, the neighbors circulated a petition to force them to move out, but were not successful. After my mother passed away in 2009, my husband, my four-year-old son and I moved into the house. [When I joined the NESG I was] working with a nonprofit organization called the Los Angeles County Children's Planning Council (CPC) (now the Children's Council of Los Angeles County). [At the time] the CPC was in the early stages of developing its community engagement approach, and trying to figure out how to engage leadership from both service organizations and local communities in order to further the well-being of children and families in LA County. During the first two years, NESG served mainly as a learning and reflection space for me. . . . We discussed issues around education and learned to utilize organizing tools, such as one-to-ones. We had mini-training sessions on leadership, power, self-interest, and on understanding our own stories of why we did our work as educators, organizers, or service providers. (Excerpted from Castillo's story in Avila, 2010, pp. 46–49)

IAF organizers often led the training mentioned by Castillo. This was a deliberate strategy on the part of the NESG to create a regional network that could have the power to partner with Occidental for the long term, by having access to ongoing community organizing training and by being connected to an organization with a city-wide leadership and power base. This was meant to address the power differential between campus and those with whom they partner in the community, a very common occurence in civic engagement. During my years at Occidental, we worked with several One LA organizers and the local IAG organization. We also worked with NESG member institutions, most of whom became paying members of One LA through the CCBL. Occidental was one of these NESG members. Castillo and others also attended a 10-day IAF national training and participated in several political actions related to education. Surya Kalra, one of the Occidental students involved with the NESG, was employed by NESG members as a part-time organizer after graduating. She later became a professional IAF organizer.

Finding and developing leaders take a great deal of intentionality, persistence, and many one-to-one meetings. In the following, Alexis Moreno, who was also a community partner of the CCBL and assistant director until 2008, comments on the labor-intensive, relational, and slow process of finding leaders with a clear vision of what really matters to them—their self-interest. She was one of the community partners who attended IA's summer organizing institute in 2013.

> Before we built this group of leaders [NESG], I had to work on reweaving the relationship between the college and community organizations. One of the core institutions in the area is Franklin High School, about a mile and a half away from Occidental. In years past, the two schools had enjoyed a healthy and cooperative relationship, which included Franklin students getting scholarships to attend Occidental. This relationship was ruptured a few years before CCBL was founded, but I didn't know this. All I knew was that there was no connection and I was determined to make one. I met with about 8 to 10 stakeholders at Franklin (teachers, parents, administrators, union reps) before I found one person who was interested in being part of the group. His name is Luis Lopez, and he was the principal and a Franklin as well as an Oxy alum. He also lived in the area. But most importantly, he had a clear sense of his path, and how his education at both Franklin and Oxy helped him create a good life. And he was clear that he wanted to create this for his students. (Moreno, personal communication, fall 2013)

After finding this new leader for the NESG whose self-interest Moreno had identifed, a process of assessment for Franklin's principal and the rest of the NESG members ensued to determine whether this would in fact be a good match for the long-term work we were trying to do around access and equity. I remember, for instance, the first time Lopez joined an NESG meeting. Upon observing the relational and reflective format of the meeting, he expressed his frustration about the slow pace of our approach to figuring out a long-term strategy to create what by then had become our charge, a college-going culture in northeast Los Angeles. He wondered why we were not simply looking at models used in other cities, known as best practices, which we could then try to replicate in our region. This opened a discussion where one by one the faculty and community leaders present that day explained their interest in building something based on people who were clear about their interests and passions, the things that matter to them deeply and enough to sustain their involvement over time. This and other moments where my coleaders, not I, explained the organizing approach to our work, and did so with ownership, signaled the way in which we were creating an organizing, relational culture through collective leadership.

Nick Orlando, who became Rodriguez's second-in-command at PUC, describes one specific example of the relational culture Rodriguez and his staff learned at the NESG. In the following story, Orlando illustrates some of the steps he and others at the school where he was principal at the time went through in developing such a culture, as well as one specific outcome of this process.

> We decided a few years ago to shift the concept of *parent involvement* to *parent engagement*. Our first initiative at CALS [middle school] proved to be a culture-shifting experience. Before the new school year started, we met with incoming parents and asked them, "What is your vision for your child, and what do you want [his or her] relationship with [the] teacher to be like?" We also asked the teachers the same types of questions. Most responses from parents were aligned with those of the teachers, with a focus on college success for the children and a safe environment for learning. Our gap analysis, however, found that parents just wanted to "know who they (the teachers) were." Our teachers had not given responses around relationship-building with parents in a way that allowed parents to get to know them personally. In response to these findings, teachers at CALS now engage in relationship-building activities that enable the parents, students, and teachers to learn about each other. This relationship-building between teachers and parents allowed us to move to the next step, that of engaging parents in the school and in the achievement of all students, not just their own children. The guidance and support of One LA helped us advance to this next level, strengthening our parent meetings with one-to-ones, and creating a core set of parents who were able to share, make decisions, and engage in school growth and decision making. Our parents have now been a part of creating our Expected School-Wide Learning Results program, which leads new parents through orientations and "relationship-building nights" for the school. At these events, parents sit side-by-side with teachers to brainstorm, reflect, and design. (Avila, 2010, p. 54)

There were many other leaders, such as Freer, Rodriguez, Orlando, Castillo, and Moreno, who were engaged in a deep, long-term campus-community collaborative. These leaders and I learned, reflected, and took action together, and we together grew in our personal and professional development.

Practice 3: Understanding and Using Power

Through this third organizing practice we were able to ensure that strategies and programming at the CCBL and related to the NESG were based on an analysis of power dynamics within the campus and in the external communities. In the early stages of the relational work at Occidental it became apparent to me and to those with whom I was working closely that in this institution faculty, and tenured in particular, were key in the power structure. This realization did not come to us as the result of a formal power analysis, such as that described in chapter 2. Rather, it came to us in countless individual and group conversations with faculty who were central in developing the charge of the CCBL with me during the first year. In other words, power analysis can be a formal, intentional activity on an as-needed basis, as well as integrated into regular conversations and meetings, also as needed. Thus, through this ongoing discussion about power dynamics and their implications for the CCBL, we learned that, compared to administrators and students, faculty tend to stay the longest at the college and that their tenured status gives them job protection. Treating tenure-track and tenured faculty as key in the creation of the CCBL also made sense because the CCBL's charge was to create curriculum-based community engagement. Nevertheless, we paid attention to the views and interests of the senior administration and academic support program directors as well, as they are undeniably part of the institutional power structure.

Analyzing power dynamics on a regular basis also helped us stay relevant and realistic with our work, which speaks to the pragmatist aspect of this practice. Faculty leaders with whom I worked the closest in envisioning and creating the CCBL understood their power positions within the college based on whether and to what extent they were respected by the administration and their peers. These faculty members were also familiar with the power structure of the institution, which was helpful as they became part of the faculty CCBL committee, such as in the case of Freer. An important factor that that was realized from our power discussions for our work at the time, for instance, was the fact that Mitchell was still fairly new as president. As a result faculty, who often have an adversarial relationship with senior administrators, seemed open to his vision of creating an engaged campus. As a newcomer to higher education, it was also important for me to learn about the very common fighting for limited financial resources present in most higher education campuses. This became a key part of conversations with the new dean of the college and vice president of academic affairs (provost, on other campuses) hired in 2004, who expressed his interest in moving the CCBL from the president's office to his. As time progressed, our power analysis conversations always included updates on institutional finances, especially since we always needed to make decisions on program development based on information about institutional budgetary priorities.

As civically engaged scholars, faculty with whom I was closely working were also aware of power structures and dynamics outside of the campus. Similarly, the community partners who became part of the NESG were leaders whose vision in connection to their professional roles was based on values and practices to create better conditions in their communities, but these leaders were also aware of and knowledgeable about the power dynamics affecting their institutions and communities and the college. In the following, Castillo explains how her understanding of power evolved, and how in the process she taught this to others with whom she was working through her organization.

> In 2006, after close to three years with NESG I attended an IAF 10-day, community organizing national training. The IAF training was significant for me because during that training I realized that I had always avoided engaging with power, both as an individual and as a professional. I learned that engaging power is different from confronting power or questioning authority. I had confronted power before, but I had also intentionally avoided doing so because I did not trust people in powerful positions and did not think there was any space to engage power. I had made assumptions about people in power and did not see the point of asking what . . . [were their interests] . . . or communicating to them about what I and others in my community cared about and were interested in being part of, such as the education of our children. The training, however, reminded me that this type of conversation could occur if there was a collective of organized institutions and people. However, not all [of the parents and organizations I was working with] knew the NESG and vice versa, so at our March 2007 NESG meeting we hosted a joint meeting, which then became a series of joint meetings held every 2 months, at various schools throughout Northeast Los Angeles. The goal of these meetings was to prepare for a community meeting with the newly elected school board member for the area, Yolie Flores Aguilar. (Excerpted from Castillo's story in Avila, 2010, pp. 49–50)

Castillo's conflict with the concept of power in connection with her development as a leader is very common in our society, as illustrated in chapter 2 (Alinsky, 1971; Gecan, 2002). The meeting with the newly elected Los Angeles board member she mentions was an action that came after a year of training and discussions about power in the NESG. The actual action was a culmination of this process of collective learning and decision-making. That the meeting succeeded in establishing a relationship of power with the board member is an important victory. However, I consider the most important victory coming out of this action the education we received about our own individual and collective power. This to me is democracy in the making, and a significant aspect of creating a culture of collective leadership by learn-ing together and taking action together.

Alan Knoerr offers a faculty perspective about his awareness of the role of power in his committee service at Occidental. He says that when he joined Occidental's mathematics department in 1991 his colleagues had a passion to change undergraduate mathematics education so that mathematics would become more widely accessible. Then, he says, "10 years later, following a series of retirements, and other institutional changes, this program had largely faded. I realized that I did not know enough about how power and institutions worked to be able to institutionalize changes I had helped bring about" (Avila, 2010, pp. 55–56). He then talks about attending an NESG meeting and deciding to try the organizing practices he had observed at this meeting in his faculty committee work. Knoerr did much more than attend that meeting. He became a long-term member of the CCBL faculty com-mittee and of the NESG. Most importantly, he committed to his own edu-cation and development as a faculty and community leader who is aware of the role of power in the long-term sustainability of his civically engaged work, thus becoming what Harry Boyte (2013) calls a *civic professional*. Over time, Knoerr's work led to his involvement as a key leader in creating a Los Angeles chapter of the Algebra Project, the national organization founded by civil rights leader Bob Moses, which focuses on mathematics as a social justice issue.

Knoerr also led the process of developing a partnership between Occi-dental's math department and Franklin High School, after learning from Franklin's school principal at NESG meetings that many students have prob-lems passing Algebra 1. Failing Algebra 1 keeps many students from graduat-ing, thus denying those students access to higher education. This, for Knoerr, became a significant social justice issue. Here is his account of how this part-nership evolved in reciprocity with three of his colleagues at Occidental and with teachers and administrators at Franklin High School:

> Throughout the 2005–2006 academic year, three colleagues in Occiden-tal's Math Department and I met collectively and individually with math teachers and administrators at Franklin. We spoke of our interests and listened to each other. In the end, we decided our students would benefit from interacting with each other. We also decided we wanted to continue our faculty-to-faculty collaboration. Together we designed a new course, Math 201: Mathematics, Education, and Access to Power. This is a small seminar course taught at Occidental College every semester, with an aver-age enrollment of six students. There are no specific prerequisites. The course meets once a week. We read and discuss papers on the cognitive sci-ence, pedagogy, and politics of mathematics education. Students also work

each week with students and teachers at Franklin or other local schools. The course culminates in individual or group projects with the schools. Students' participation is informed by the course readings, and by what they have learned through their community work. Occidental students have found this to be a life-changing course, with a significant proportion deciding afterward to become involved in social justice work, and even to become math teachers. The schools have also benefited in many ways. The success of Math 201 encouraged us to deepen our involvement. Faculty discussions supported an experiment at Franklin that involved comparing two alternative curricula to the traditional one. Franklin ultimately adopted a vastly superior mathematics curriculum. (Avila, 2010, pp. 57–58)

Knoerr adds that throughout the development of this and other partnerships, the four organizing practices described in chapter 2 were used intentionally, and that the collective goal was to learn together about how to improve math education. Knoerr and others in the partnership learned about their motivations for participating in this partnership, which became a multiyear collaboration and grew to include other public schools in northeast Los Angeles and beyond. These stakeholders shared a passion for equity and access, which they learned about in the process of working together. This partnership and other NESG and CCBL meetings became cocreative, reciprocal spaces where parts of our personal narratives were often shared, to deepen our individual and collective civic agency. Here Knoerr gives a brief synopsis of his narrative, which helps clarify the origins of his interest in social justice through his civically engaged scholarship:

I grew up in Durham, North Carolina, and attended segregated public schools. When I was in junior high school the system integrated and I went to Hillside, the traditionally African American high school in the city. Largely due to a remarkable meeting of minds between C. P. Ellis, a local Ku Klux Klan leader, and Ann Atwater, a Black civil rights activist, integration did for a time lead to genuine engagement between Blacks and Whites in Durham. As a teenager, I was able to see that remarkable social change can occur when people start working together. (Avila, 2010, p. 56)

While the previous three organizing practices helped find leaders, build a collective of leadership, and develop strategies based on an understanding of power dynamics, the sustainability of this work was underpinned by ongoing critical reflection. This type of reflection often led us to share stories such as Freer's, Rodriguez's, Castillo's, and Knoerr's, thus helping us reground our work on our self- and collective interests.

Practice 4: Ongoing Critical Reflection

The discipline of reflecting on an ongoing basis was part of the entire process of creating the work of the CCBL. With time, faculty members, students, and community leaders with whom I worked closely joined me in integrating this practice in everything we did together. These reflective moments often included updating ourselves on institutional and community power dynamics, assessing our progress, and identifying stakeholders with whom we might need to do one-to-one meetings. Thus, we engaged in critical reflection during all meetings, and prior to and immediately after all events, including the summer CBL/CBR workshops, CCBL faculty committee meetings, staff meetings, NESG meetings, and student-engaged projects. This ongoing critical reflection ensured that our work stayed relevant and effective, and that we based our strategies and activities on reality, rather than on unchecked assumptions. Equally important, however, reflection helped us build trust and collective ownership, and it affirmed and reaffirmed our values, knowledge, and resources. It also helped us define clear, realistic terms of accountability and respect among ourselves.

One of the most powerful moments I remember, which emerged from this type of reflection, trust, and ongoing one-to-ones and power analyses, happened in 2006, as NESG members were discussing the implications of the ending of a grant that funded Alexis Moreno's job for the future of our collective work. This was a moment of tension for several reasons. Moreno had become key in the work of the NESG, and the CCBL's staff and faculty committee were trying to negotiate for her job to become institutionalized during the first semester of a newly hired college president. We calculated that we had a gap of a couple of months between the end of her salary and the time we thought it would take for the president to give us a final decision. To everyone's surprise, Rodriguez responded to this dilemma by offering funds from his organization to pay for these two months of Moreno's salary. Many years later, this memory is still charged with emotions for me. To me this is not about shaming the college or the president or about anger because the college was relinquishing its responsibility by allowing Rodriguez's organization to spend its limited resources in this way. Neither is this about romanticizing Rodriguez's charitable gesture. Rather, I view this as an example of a true covenant; of a social contract; and an example of what organized, relational power can do. This is a deeper level of reciprocity than most of us usually practice in the field of academic civic engagement.

The following semester, at an NESG meeting to engage with this new president, we told this story to illustrate what we meant by partnerships between the college and the community. This happened after we had succeeded in securing institutional funds for Moreno's position. After hearing the story, the president expressed gratitude to Rodriguez, while recognizing his commitment to this level of engagement. I still remember Rodriguez's answer. He simply said, "Oh, believe me, this was all about my self-interest in protecting the work of the NESG!"

Assessing Success and Challenges

I summarize in this section some of our most important accomplishments, as well as challenges we faced.

What We Accomplished

One example of measuring interest in CBL throughout the campus occurred during the early stages of the CCBL. We wanted to find ways to learn the extent to which this topic was discussed even when our staff and faculty leaders were not present. This instance became apparent when we began to hear from faculty members who were not part of the CCBL leadership that CBL (integrating civic engagement in the classroom) was being discussed at various campus-wide meetings. Knowing that CBL was of interest to the campus community meant that the movement had momentum and a growing base.

A second example of measuring progress took place between 2005 and 2010, when a large number of new faculty members were hired. At the request of the CCBL faculty committee, the dean of the college made an announcement to all faculty regarding departmental proposals requesting new faculty positions. He asked faculty to consider including CBL experience or interest in all searches for new faculty. Shortly after this announcement, our staff and faculty leaders approached the chairs of the various faculty searches and offered guidance regarding what would count as CBL/CBR experience or interest. These two efforts were successful, and starting in 2005, the CCBL became part of the itinerary for interviews of most finalist candidates for new faculty positions. This became a way for new faculty to become part of those we invited to our annual summer workshops, and thus a way to help them integrate CBL/CBR into their scholarship.

A third example of assessing progress is illustrated through Education in Action (EIA), a program through which students were hired and trained to assist faculty with CBL classes and CBR projects. The program was cocreated in 2004 by a team of about 10 students; one English faculty professor; a faculty member teaching diversity-related courses; the director of the Center for Religious and Spiritual Life; the director of the Multicultural Center; and myself, the director of CCBL. As part of creating this program, the students attended a training at the Center for Democracy and Citizenship at the University of Minnesota (currently at Augsburg College), based on the center's Public Achievement program. After trying EIA in three courses for a year, all these stakeholders realized that this program was worth keeping, but that it would require sustained funding to pay stipends to EIA student facilitators. We together decided that it would be best to house this program in the CCBL, and we met with the dean of the college to obtain this required funding. As a result of that meeting, EIA facilitators are paid a stipend, are selected by the faculty whom they will be assisting and by the CCBL director, and work 10 to 15 hours weekly. "Through the program, facilitators expand their role as students, build leadership skills, and further develop their understanding of social justice and responsibility" (Castillo et al., 2015, p. 293).

Veronica Toledo, an Occidental alumna and former EIA student, offered the following testimonial about her experience in this program.

> I am currently working with Professor Castaneda in the Education Department through the CCBL. Professor Castaneda is conducting research with Latina mothers in South Gate, encouraging them to document their educational experiences through photography. The women take a photo each week related to a specific topic such as "Family and Education" and then meet to discuss what they have captured. Through such discussions, they are identifying a number of common concerns such as the need for tutoring, stronger after-school programs, and a cleaner campus. Parents are not merely discussing such issues, but also developing creative solutions. For example, the women recently proposed a family festival that would engage parents in a school cleanup, while also connecting parents through games, food, art classes for the children, and so on. Such recommendations will be provided to the school and the publication of such research will further demonstrate the importance of parent involvement in transforming education. Through this experience with the CCBL, I have discovered my passion for education, community organizing, and parent engagement. I am now applying to organizations dedicated to these areas. (Personal communication, August 17, 2014)

After graduation, Veronica obtained a job with the Green Dot charter schools as a parent organizer. Veronica shared this testimonial after participating in a CCBL gathering of faculty, EIA students, and their community partners. Castillo, CCBL's director, recently shared that this type of gathering has become an annual event.

Castillo and colleagues give a more recent student testimonial, which came from regular reflections students are required to write about their experience. This student, Benyapa B., who had been an EIA facilitator for three semesters, wrote that her work as an EIA facilitator "has exposed me to ways of initiating thoughtful and effective community-based research." She adds that she has "gained an increasingly developed sense of social responsibility and change." She continues: "While the nature of the CBR projects proved challenging and I continue to grapple with privilege and power, my experience has been extremely rewarding and I am thankful for the opportunity to engage in [CBL]" (Castillo et al., 2015, p. 294).

The most important aspect for us at the CCBL in this program was to help EIA facilitators be in control of their education, and in turn help students in the classes where they were assisting do the same.

A fourth example of assessing progress is the way in which faculty's scholarship was transformed. Spanish professor Felisa Guillen is one such example. To Guillen, CBL, or *service-learning* as she calls it, is about much more than integrating this pedagogy in a few courses. She tells the story about integrating CBL in the Spanish department in her article "Including Latino Communities in the Learning Process: Curricular and Pedagogical Reforms in Undergraduate Spanish Programs," published by the *Journal of Community Engagement and Scholarship*. In her words:

> We chose not to conceptualize service-learning in terms of individual course design only, but to explore its potential as a vehicle of curricular reform (Zlotkowski, 2001). Therefore, instead of offering one or two courses with a service-learning emphasis, we decided to completely adopt this teaching model and to work together as a department toward the incorporation of service-learning across the Spanish curriculum. (Guillen, 2012)

I remember Guillen approaching me in the morning of the second day of one of the CCBL's early summer CBL workshops. She was moved and energized by the workshop, and this had given her a vision to take what she was learning in the workshop to her department. She knew then that she wanted to teach her classes using this approach, and she also knew that she wanted to integrate this throughout her department. But, she cautioned in the following, making the transition to CBL teaching was not easy:

> After so many years of individual work, it wasn't easy having to change my previous model and relinquish some of the control that I used to have over my classes and activities. For instance, I had to learn to work collaboratively, taking into account the student's input; relying on other people's expertise, such as the director and staff from the CCBL; and making room for the community in the teaching and learning process. (Castillo et al., 2015, p. 293)

A fifth example of success is an attempt to integrate CBL and CBR into the Faculty Handbook, with specific language for valuing and rewarding this type of scholarship. This language was presented to the Faculty Council (Occidental's faculty government body), but final approval was interrupted by a series of administrative changes, starting with Ted Mitchell's resignation in 2005. While this effort did not succeed during my tenure, the CCBL hosted workshops and several faculty discussions on the topic, which often included administrators and members of the Advisory Council committee, the committee that reviews for reappointment, tenure, and promotion. These workshops and discussions did, eventually, make it easier for CBL and CBR to count toward tenure and promotion.

A sixth and more standard example of assessing progress was manifested when Occidental College was awarded the President's Higher Education Community Service Honor Roll with Distinction for exemplary service efforts in 2009, for the fifth consecutive year, and when it was selected for the 2008 Community Engagement Elective Classification in the category of Curricular Engagement and Outreach and Partnerships, by the Carnegie Foundation for the Advancement of Teaching.

As a final example of success, and related to the CCBL's presence in the surrounding communities, in March 2009 the NESG was recognized by the Los Angeles Board of Education for its contribution to the education of students in the Los Angeles Unified School District. The award document states, "The Los Angeles Board of Education and the Superintendent express their appreciation to the Northeast Education Strategies Group for their outstanding contribution to the students of the Los Angeles Unified School District." This type of award has served as evidence of how the work of the center has influenced the communities and the educational political structure surrounding the college.

Having shared my assessment of the success of the work of the CCBL, I share now my assessment of some of the challenges we encountered.

Challenges We Faced

First, because this model is founded on the ongoing relational and reflective process and methodology given previously, it was a challenge at times to do this type of work in our predominant culture of wanting quick, concrete, predictable results, and in a culture that undervalues process and relationality.

Second, I experienced tension between my organizer role in creating a community of key leaders within and across participating stakeholder groups and the more traditional approach, which would place the staff/director as the only or main public face of the CCBL. This at times confused college administrators, who expected to see me "at all tables" where academic civic engagement was being discussed. For example, one faculty member who was very supportive of the CCBL told me once that some senior administrators said that I was having faculty do my job for me, and said it as if I was at fault. In reality, as I have explained, I was guiding this process for faculty ownership and long-term sustainability of the CCBL.

Third, and relatedly, this approach often created political friction with senior administration because it focused on creating institutional ownership with faculty. As we observed, the main reason for this friction is that new administrators come with their own interests and visions for the college which often differ from our collective leadership-based, relational, and strategic approach. The culture of academia has an ongoing element of tension and distrust between administration and faculty. Tenured faculty in the United States, for instance, often have a significant level of immunity regarding disciplinary actions, and this can lead to lack of accountability toward each other and toward other stakeholders within and outside the institution. Administrators, however, seem to have their own sense of entitlement by virtue of their access to and control of institutional resources. My administrative position was middle management, which meant that my direct line of supervision came from the administration, yet the faculty committee had a very deep sense of ownership of my work and, therefore, direct involvement in program implementation and assessment. As a result, faculty sometimes stepped in to protect my work and also the work of the CCBL, but obviously this was not always welcomed by the administration. Making the importance of ownership by all stakeholders explicit to the administration often lessened this tension, but this became a challenge as we had to do this with every one of the five presidents and deans of the college we had during the 10 years of my tenure at Occidental.

Fourth, the primary focus on faculty ownership placed the CCBL in academic affairs, causing tension with student affairs staff, who at Occidental had a history of working primarily in cocurricular community engagement. Student affairs senior administrators often tried to move the CCBL out of academic affairs and into student affairs, based on what often seemed to be a desire to increase their influence and power reach, possibly combined with a genuine interest in and their own philosophy of civic engagement.

A fifth challenge and limitation surfaced during the interviews I did in the summer of 2013. This limitation relates to the extent to which the approach we used at Occidental, and academic civic engagement in general, addresses issues of institutional culture change regarding diversity on our campuses. The specific question is whether the community organizing approach we used is appropriate for organizing on diversity-related issues. Ultimately this challenge raises the question of how we define *institutional culture change*, as well as a larger question regarding the intersection between civic engagement and diversity. This is something I have become more aware of and continue to learn about with other colleagues, but an understanding of how to do this intentionally and strategically is still not clear to many of us.

Summarizing Accomplishments

Reflecting about our accomplishments and challenges during my tenure at Occidental, I am left with a deep sense of personal and professional growth, and much, much gratitude toward all who joined me in this journey. The most important of all accomplishments, in my assessment, is the fact that we created a culture that values and rewards reciprocal civic engagement, throughout the disciplines, on and off campus. Partly because this culture became institutionalized, but particularly because of the group of faculty who came to own the work of the CCBL as their own, it continues to exist as I write this book (spring 2017), surviving various administrations and their various agendas regarding civic engagement, and my own departure from the college in 2011. This type of culture change was our overall goal, and I believe that using community organizing was the reason that this took place. This is significant especially in light of the challenging context in which civic engagement continues to exist. It is also significant because we created spaces where various civic engagement stakeholders came together in long-term sustained conversations and deliberation about what matters to them, their institutions, and their communities. This often led them to take action to create culture change, such as the examples given by Rodriguez, Orlando, Guillen, Freer, Toledo, Knoerr, and Castillo.

Many of the faculty, students, and community partners who were part of the collective of leadership at Occidental have continued being part of creating new collaboratives through my work at USC, with IA, and at CSUDH. Many also played a significant role through my doctoral studies. I want to be clear, in ending this reflection, that this transformation of the culture of the college does not mean that every faculty member and student became involved in reciprocal civically engaged scholarship, or that we transformed the communities surrounding the college. I do want to assert, however, that the concept and practice of reciprocal civically engaged scholarship became widely known throughout campus, and with those with whom CCBL classes partnered. The story of what the CCBL did at Occidental is meant to show that this type of culture transformation can happen, but also that this is a slow, intentional, and strategic process. It took us 10 years to transform the culture, but as evidenced by the recent stories included in this chapter, it continues strong. A very significant element in our success in changing the culture of the college was the consistent and continuous role of faculty, particularly through the formalization of the CCBL's work in faculty governance. As of January 2017, the description of this committee reads as follows:

Community-Based Learning and Research Committee: *Regina Freer (chair)*

This committee focuses on enhancing curriculum-connected community engagement and community-based research. . . . This committee works with the Center for Community-Based Learning (CCBL) to provide guidance on faculty development and support needed for faculty to implement and sustain community-based learning within their courses and research, often serving as peer mentors. This group examines and makes recommendations for policies related to community-based learning to other college committees and constituencies. (Occidental College, n.d.)

I have continued experimenting with the four organizing practices illustrated in this chapter in other contexts, while creating spaces similar to those that we created at Occidental, in various and different contexts.

4

THE MARKET, CIVICALLY
ENGAGED SCHOLARSHIP,
AND RECIPROCITY

I t is clear that there is an interest and a commitment from many academics, students, and administrators regarding public, civically engaged
scholarship, and that this scholarship is viewed as part of higher education's moral and social responsibility to society. And we know that many
organizations, institutions, and groups outside of academia are interested in
joining this endeavor. We know this from experience as engaged students,
staff, faculty, and administrators, as well as from the many publications in
the field. We know it, too, from the many national and even international
organizations that promote this type of scholarship, such as IA, Campus
Compact, Community-Campus Partnerships for Health, and the Talloires
Network, just to name a few.

I have given detailed examples of such cases at Occidental and through
my work with IA. In this chapter, I share views and experiences about civically engaged scholarship and the context in which it operates, from my
doctoral research at Maynooth University and from my postdoctoral research
at USC. My research at these two institutions is not the focus of this chapter,
however. Rather, the views and experiences of academics, administrators, and
community partners are shared here to illustrate the influence of the market
in higher education, its effects in creating a culture that rewards civically
engaged scholarship, and the creation of reciprocal community-campus partnerships. As I share the views and experiences from interviews at Maynooth
and USC, I will name individuals only when they have clearly authorized
me to do so and otherwise will refer to them by their professional roles and
institutions.

Maynooth and USC Research Summary

To offer some institutional and geographical context, I give here brief descriptions of Maynooth and USC.

Maynooth University

The primary purpose of my doctoral research at Maynooth was to explore views and experiences regarding civically engaged scholarship at that institution, within the larger context of the role that the university could and should play in its surrounding region. A secondary purpose was to explore whether the four organizing practices I used at Occidental could aid in this project. That is, if these practices worked at Maynooth, this could lead to institutionalizing civically engaged scholarship. At the time of my research, many academics in various disciplines were engaged with their surrounding communities in a number of ways, but the concept of civic engagement or civically engaged scholarship was not widely known. I had in-depth interviews with faculty from various disciplines, senior administrators, and community partners. I also had several group meetings mostly with faculty and administrators, where we would discuss key aspects of what I was learning through interviews in the context of whether a movement could emerge in support of institutionalizing civic engagement. These discussions included themes relevant to institutional power dynamics and financial aspects, such as the search for a new president and the loss of public funding for higher education in general and for Maynooth in particular.

Two specific events came out of this process, which led to the creation of a collective of academics who continued meeting about ways to institutionalize civic engagement (not focused only on civically engaged scholarship) at Maynooth. First, my research culminated in March 2011 with a meeting hosted by then-president Tom Collins, attended by 16 academics from various disciplines. At this meeting, an academic from digital humanities and one from sociology spoke about their engaged work, in the context of the role of the university in the region and in Irish society in general. These two academics were joined by the director of the Office of Commercialization, who spoke about how his office engages with the business and the government sectors. President Collins led the discussion after the three presentations. After this meeting, several academics made a decision to continue meeting and strategizing about institutionalizing civic engagement on their campus. They planned, for example, a meeting to strategize about how to gain support from the upcoming university president.

Second, and in continuation of the planning this group of academics did after the culmination of my research, the group organized a campus-wide gathering, with a focus on discussing civic engagement at Maynooth, and invited their new president. This meeting took place a day after my dissertation defense (known as *viva* in Ireland), in February 2012, and I was asked to give a brief, framing talk for the event. The president seemed seriously interested and engaged in the conversations at this gathering. I know from anecdotal accounts a year after this gathering that a staff position had been created to coordinate civic engagement activities, but I do not think the focus was on civically engaged scholarship. Yet, my research project did create a space for academics to learn together and collaborate on discussions and strategizing around civic engagement. The excerpts from interviews I share in this chapter (either direct excerpts or clarified in follow-up interviews) illustrate the deep level at which they engaged with me. This is also how they engaged with each other at the various group discussions we had during my doctoral research. That this much was accomplished is significant, especially given the fact that my PhD was research based. As a result, I was traveling from Los Angeles to Maynooth once per semester, from January 2009 through March 2011, specifically for interviews and meetings with my advisers (called *supervisors* in Ireland).

USC

The purpose of my postdoctoral research at USC was similar to my research at Maynooth. The difference was that USC has a very long history of civically engaged scholars. USC's JEP has been instrumental in this history during its 40 years of existence. Because this is a large institution, there are a number of other programs, centers, and departments that offer support to students and faculty interested in engaging with non-campus communities. These programs include the Civic Engagement Initiative in the Sol Price School of Policy, Community Outreach in the Keck School of Medicine, the Center for Environmental and Regional Equity, and the Center for Diversity and Democracy, to name a few. The focus of my interviews with civically engaged faculty was to explore interest in institutionalizing civically engaged teaching and research in the curriculum in addition to exploring views and experience with civically engaged scholarship. This topic emerged from preliminary interviews and from conversations with my mentor and adviser, George Sanchez.

In individual interviews and in group discussions I learned that while civically engaged scholarship was not uncommon, there was no consensus on what *civically engaged teaching and research* meant, and civically engaged courses were not clearly designated as such in the curriculum. I saw this as a topic around which to bring faculty together in conversation. Similar to my methods at Maynooth, I interviewed community partners about their views and experiences of engagement with USC faculty, as well as about whether institutionalizing this type of scholarship would benefit them as partners. There were several individual and group discussions with faculty, and several individual and one group discussion with community partners. Two events point to actions that emerged from this process.

First, in March 2014, my last semester at USC, I held a meeting with about 15 faculty members from various disciplines, which focused on creating a civic engagement minor as a way to institutionalize civically engaged teaching and research in the curriculum. While there was sufficient interest to pursue this idea, the ending of my fellowship ended this project. Second, in July 2014, the Center for Diversity and Democracy hosted a gathering where several community partners and faculty who were part of this project came together in conversation about their views and experiences regarding the role USC has and can play in the surrounding communities, particularly through teaching and research.

This meeting was the culmination of my research. The conversations were very rich, and several participants commented that there are not enough opportunities for community partners and faculty to engage in conversation with one another. Those in attendance expressed interest in continuing the conversation, with possibilities for reciprocal collaborations emerging from this process. I don't think this idea was pursued, however, most likely because of lack of staff at the center to ensure this would happen. Like at Maynooth, my research project did succeed in creating spaces for collaborations around civically engaged scholarship; unlike at Maynooth, at USC faculty and community partners actually came together on this topic, at least once.

In both cases, discussing ways in which market values have influenced how universities operate became common, particularly the pressures of doing this type of scholarship without institutional rewards toward tenure and promotion. It is also clear, thus, that while there is interest in civically engaged scholarship, there are strong currents pushing against such an endeavor. This is especially true when trying to create deep, long-term, sustainable, reciprocal partnerships that emerge from collective civic agency, which aim to create culture change in and outside academia. Much of these strong currents are underpinned by a market culture that values profit making and individualism over human rights and collective, participatory civic agency. This theme also recurred through my collaborations with IA and the Kettering Foundation. And yet, this is a topic that has not been openly, intentionally, and strategically addressed in the movement of civic engagement.

Academic senior administrators talk about their institutional financial challenges and solutions, and faculty talk about the way in which their scholarship and academic departments are rewarded based on the amount of external research grants and revenue from student enrollment. Many directors of civic engagement offices are painfully aware of the underfunded and understaffed conditions in which they operate. Students, for the most part, see the university primarily as a place to get a degree that will lead to better economic conditions. Community partners, for the most part, are unaware of these conditions inside academia and often expect much more sharing of the resources they assume universities have, while struggling to meet their own organizational financial demands. Rarely, if at all, have I seen spaces where all these stakeholders meet to understand the larger forces that are behind all of their predicaments.

The Market and Higher Education: Neoliberalism

Lisa Duggan (2007) traces the word *neoliberalism* back to the 1930s, but she states that it became most commonly used in the 1990s. She describes it in the following:

> To name a utopian ideology of "free markets" and minimal state interference, a set of policies slashing state social services and supporting global corporate interests, a process (neoliberalization) proceeding in company with procorporate globalization and financialization, and a cultural project of building consent for the upward redistributions of wealth and power that have occurred since the 1970s. But neoliberalism might best be understood as a global social movement encompassing all of these political goals. (p. 45)

In this context, Giroux (2015), Lynch (2008), and Newfield (2011) establish a connection between this movement and what they perceive as the crisis of higher education. Lynch (2008) further asserts that "in this new market state, the individual (rather than the nation) is held responsible for her or his own well-being. The state's role is one of facilitator and enabler of the consumer and market-led citizen" (p. 3), arguing that those who favor neoliberalism have a view of citizenship as market based, which is against citizens' rights to education as a state guarantee. In this scenario, Lynch argues, education is delivered by the market only to those who can afford it.

These changes in higher education's purpose, according to Newfield (2011), are not accidental. Rather, he sees these changes as a conservative 40-year-old campaign against higher education's influence in democratizing U.S. society. This, he argues, is a threat to access to higher education, and thus a threat to the U.S. middle class.

In an article in the *Los Angeles Times* titled "The Big Business of College 'Naming Opportunities,'" Gottlieb (1999) describes another aspect of how universities serve corporate interests:

> It took $35 million from the fortune of aerospace company founder Gordon Marshall to persuade USC to name its business school after him. Forty-five million dollars from the Gonda family put their name on UCLA's Neuroscience and Genetics Research Center. . . . But they have nothing on furnace company founder Henry Rowan. For his $100 million, Glassboro State College in New Jersey was re-christened Rowan College.

The article continues: "'You name it, we'll name it,' said Paul Blodgett, associate vice president for university relations at USC, where a street light goes for $15,000."

This issue of serving corporate interests and its effect on universities' business model, real as it is, is far from straightforward, and we often don't think about the financial realities that may play a role in administrators' and academics' conforming to the market's interest. These words from a former Maynooth University president (interviewed in the spring semester of 2010) give a glimpse of these realities:

> What's happening in Ireland is that [the university's] autonomy has been wiped out because of financial problems. I've been told we can't hire and we can't fire. I have no control over income because we can't increase fees. . . . I have no control over expenditures because salaries are fixed by the government. . . . What kind of autonomy do we have?

A related, well-known fact is the shrinking government funding for higher education, both in Ireland and in the United States, and this is another reason given by administrators and academics for partnering with the business sector for funding opportunities. Thus, although this president is obviously frustrated with government interference with the autonomy of the university, he is nonetheless enthusiastic about what others might see as interference from multinational corporations. This is what he said about the university's partnership with Intel, which is located near the university:

> We now manage Intel Foundation's work in Ireland . . . and distribute funding to local schools and community organizations. . . . Intel are very influential in setting policy here because they are such a huge investor. . . . They have an iconic image because they are a big American company. [For this reason] when the chairman of Intel came to give a talk in Ireland, at my

invitation, I wrote to the Taoiseach [prime minister] to inform him, and he agreed to meet with the chairman. [Also] when the minister for enterprise trades and investment was formulating its plan for the knowledge society and so on, it was myself and people from Intel he met with to talk about the model we have here, and that has given me the recipe to raise visibility, which would be very difficult to do by ourselves. (Personal communication, November 1, 2016)

It is clear that this university president felt justified to reach out to Intel as a way for the institution to raise its visibility within the national political structure. The model referred to in this quote has become very common in many universities, and it includes offices in charge of arranging research and funding partnerships with the business sector, often with government as a mediator. Maynooth had two such offices at the time of my doctoral research.

This market model also affects government. For instance, an elected representative I interviewed in Ireland told me that he does not trust or respect academics because they are detached from society's problems, but he was enthusiastic about universities' initiatives that use their research to help the economy through business incubation centers. His comments about universities reflect that the negative feelings expressed by former Maynooth's president toward government seem to be reciprocated; however, both agree on the importance of universities partnering with the business sector.

A paper from the Organisation for Economic Co-operation and Development (OECD; 1996), entitled "The Knowledge-Based Economy," summarizes the meaning and origin of the knowledge-based society that Maynooth's former president mentions and that the elected representative alludes to. The growing codification of knowledge and its transmission through communications and computer networks have led to the emerging *information society*. The need for workers to acquire a range of skills and to continuously adapt these skills underlies the *learning economy*. The importance of knowledge and technology diffusion requires better understanding of knowledge networks and *national innovation systems*. Most importantly, new issues and questions are being raised regarding the implications of the knowledge-based economy for employment and the role of governments in the development and maintenance of the knowledge base (OECD, 1996, p. 3).

A science academic from Maynooth gives a faculty perspective on the threat to Irish higher education (interviewed in the spring semester of 2011):

In Ireland, last year the government made an offer to U.S. companies coming here that all intellectual property generated by universities would be free for them to use. Which is unbelievable! I don't know if they really knew what they were saying. . . . That's very tragic!

A story from another Maynooth academic from the geography department illustrates a different aspect of the market's influence in higher education. This story is about a partnership between the university's academics and administrators and the community and business sectors. This faculty member is a great example of a civically engaged scholar at the local, national, and international levels. This is important to note because he had a prominent status within the university and within external communities, which can be helpful in navigating through the various sectors. This can also increase the possibilities of a positive outcome in multisector partnerships. The academic telling this story was a member of Maynooth's Community Council at the time of the partnership, and he was directly involved in this project. He told me this story in the fall of 2010, about 10 years after the incident he recounts. He starts with the intended purpose of the partnership, and then shares how the partnership, in his view, failed:

> The purpose was to prevent Maynooth from growing in a way that would affect the character of the town, as the population was growing very rapidly. This was at a time when the university was growing as well. . . . There was a sort of ethos of development [and] we were concerned [about] what was happening to services and so on. We established cooperative projects between the university and the town . . . [and] interacted with public local authorities. . . . We involved ourselves in local issues . . . [and] got involved in fair trade. . . . The main thing is that we were trying to establish a consensus among all groups to maximize benefits for the university but which also had commercial advantages without destroying the character of the town and the sense of community of the town. The partnership worked well for a while, with a lot of support from the university, but ultimately failed . . . because the objectives of the two groups clashed . . . the university and the community council. It floundered. . . . The town did not want unnecessary residential development but the university would not stand up to join them because they had several interests in expanding and selling land themselves, essentially. . . . We more or less abandoned it and we went our separate ways. What I learned is that people go into partnerships not aware that they would need to compromise on both sides and it requires a shared ethos. . . . When it comes to the crunch people will not act against their self-interest . . . but I think it is fair to say that ultimately the crunch was the inability to compromise. . . . It essentially boils down to commercial pressures . . . so the partnership model did not work here. (Personal communication, November 1, 2016)

This story is important because partnerships that involve the business sector are not very common in writings about civic engagement. It is, nonetheless, representative of a very common occurrence around many universities globally, and it is also a direct consequence of the power of the market and its values and interests and its influence in higher education. I heard similar stories, specifically related to what community residents and activists view as gentrification by the university's ongoing expansion into surrounding communities at USC. The following text from the *Los Angeles Times* describes one such example:

> Replacing a now-demolished shopping center along Jefferson Boulevard and Hoover Street, the new USC Village is to include living space for 2,700 undergraduate and graduate students in five-story residence halls, a large grocery store, a drugstore, a fitness center, restaurants and other shops. The design, all in the so-called Collegiate Gothic style that echoes much of USC's campus, surrounds a plaza that officials said they hoped would become a public gathering place. The formal groundbreaking is Monday, with the target completion date in fall 2017. The plan faced earlier opposition from some neighborhood activists about its large scale and possible effect on hastening gentrification in the area south of downtown Los Angeles. As a result, during the city's review of the 15-acre proposal, USC agreed to pay $20 million to support affordable housing in the area, among other pledges to help the neighborhood. (Gordon, 2014)

The pledges to help the neighborhood surrounding the campus came about through the efforts of a coalition of several South Los Angeles community groups, including nonprofit and faith-based organizations. I learned this through interviews with some of the leaders of these organizations, who also shared that, in their view, this partnership between this community coalition and USC succeeded by benefiting all involved, in part because the Los Angeles city government had a role as mediator. Therefore, this was a partnership among civic organizations, a private university, and government, and it was a partnership where, as told by the people I interviewed, the power and resources that all partners brought to the table were openly acknowledged in the negotiation process. As a result, the community received a financial pledge toward building affordable housing and other benefits to residents from neighborhoods near the campus, and the university was able to get the needed city permits to pursue its construction development plans. In the long term, this type of alliance can also lead to multiple long-term partnerships.

Clearly, university-business partnerships are not all negative, just as the market is not all negative, and there are many academics who appreciate the shift from government toward creating a knowledge-based society, which, in their view, has opened great opportunities for academic research to get funded and to become useful to society, such as in discovering cures for diseases. Yet others regret their lost ability to do basic research uncompromised by special interests. In this scenario, public, civically engaged, reciprocal scholarship can be challenging, especially if its practice is not formalized within the faculty rewards systems.

The Reward System and Civically Engaged Scholarship

As mentioned in chapter 1, and as Scott J. Peters's research has amply demonstrated, the history of discourses and initiatives that advocate for the formalization of civically engaged scholarship can be traced back hundreds of years, particularly through land-grant institutions (Peters, 2010; Peters & Avila, 2014). Here, I offer a brief summary of the most recent iteration of such initiatives, from the early 1980s to the present, particularly in reference to the work of Ernest Lynton. Within this period, Lynton (1983) is known as one of the first visionaries examining the gap between the practice of public service performed by faculty through their professional disciplines and the university's role in creating knowledge that is useful to society, which Driscoll and Lynton (1999) describe as

> concerns in higher education over the substantial neglect of institutional outreach and the need to reinforce the "responsibility of the university . . . to be instrumental in analyzing and applying [new] knowledge and in making it rapidly useful to all societal sectors (Lynton, 1983, p. 53)." (p. 1)

Driscoll and Lynton and many others acknowledge that these conceptions of scholarship, institutional, and faculty responsibilities gained attention and momentum after Ernest Boyer's (1990) seminal publication *Scholarship Reconsidered*. These discourses have continued, and more recent initiatives have emerged that have deepened and advanced this movement and have led to specific successes, but also show how difficult it is to formally integrate this type of scholarship into institutional reward systems.

The Tenure Team Initiative (TTI), a project of IA, led one such effort. The initiative was started in the fall of 2005, and in 2008 a report was produced entitled *Scholarship in Public: Knowledge Creation and Tenure Policy in the Engaged University: A Resource on Promotion and Tenure in the Arts, Humanities, and Design* (Ellison & Eatman, 2008). The authors acknowledge that publicly engaged scholarship has become common in many universities, yet they make a strong statement that "tenure and promotion policies lag behind public scholarly and creative work and discourage faculty from doing it" (p. 4). They continue, saying the following:

> We propose concrete ways to remove obstacles to academic work carried out for and/or with the public by giving such work full standing as

scholarship, research, or artistic creation. While we recommend a number of ways to alter the wording and intent of tenure and promotion policies, changing the rules is not enough. Enlarging the conception of who counts as "peer" and what counts as "publication" is part of something bigger: the democratization of knowledge on and off campus. (p. iv)

This "something bigger," as the authors state, has to do with creating a culture in higher education where this type of scholarship is rewarded for tenure and promotion purposes. They call on faculty, students, and administrators to join in this cause.

This report was followed by several gatherings and conversations around the country, intended to build interest and change in this regard. The Research University Civic Engagement Network (TRUCEN), created by Campus Compact in 2005, is another example of a project researching and advocating for inclusion of civically engaged scholarship in higher education's reward system. Its mission statement includes the following:

Research universities have a responsibility to help us understand our world and that understanding is enhanced through engagement with communities in solving the world's greatest problems. Those of us privileged to work in these institutions should dedicate ourselves to putting in place the structures, processes, and incentives to make it happen. It is our moral responsibility as scholars, it is our democratic responsibility as citizens, and it is our route to excellence in our scholarship and instruction. We must embrace this responsibility as an expression of our core academic, social, and civic values. (Campus Compact, 2016b)

TRUCEN evolved from a series of gatherings and conversations about the role of research universities in promoting civically engaged scholarship. From these gatherings resulted several reports that included specific lessons and recommendations, as well as a toolkit for universities interested in expanding what is viewed as traditional knowledge.

The creation of TRUCEN in 2005 and IA's report in 2008 undoubtedly influenced efforts to change tenure and reward systems in colleges and universities nationwide. This process, however, necessarily included painful moments for many academics in such institutions. Former Occidental academic Elizabeth Chin and Maria Núñez, a student who was assisting her in a gang-intervention CBL class, told one such story. In a coauthored article (Chin & Núñez, 2006), they share their views on Chin's tenure application, specifically regarding her CBL approach. According to this article, the tenure and promotion committee (Advisory Council, AC), stated that

Chin demonstrated outstanding performance in research and service, but was lacking in her teaching performance. In Professor Chin's opinion, this negative evaluation in large part resulted from the pedagogical and organizational approach required in order to best participate in a "high infusion," Community-Based Learning (CBL) experience. . . . Despite encouraging CBL projects, the AC remains skeptical of the non-traditional classroom. In Chin's fifth-year review, she was penalized for the different classroom experience she provided for students. (p. 9)

The authors conclude that such teaching pedagogies "will only truly succeed when CBL becomes institutionalized in colleges and universities, releasing professors and students into communities with the resources and support necessary for long-term success" (Chin & Núñez, 2006, p. 10). Chin's experience took place during the early years of the CCBL, and it was one case that served to galvanize faculty around this issue, thus playing an important role in progressively, but not completely, increasing institutional awareness and support of CBL and CBR. Chin shares also that this negative feedback on her CBL teaching made her aware that she needed to have prepared this section of her portfolio with anticipation of such reaction from the AC. The CCBL responded to this case by offering workshops and faculty gatherings focused on how to include CBL/CBR in tenure and promotion portfolios, and by offering individual guidance to newly hired tenure-track faculty on how to articulate their civically engaged scholarship in their tenure reports.

An example of an institution that has integrated engaged scholarship in its guidelines for tenure and promotion comes from the University of Georgia. UGA's 2014 "Guidelines for Appointment, Promotion and Tenure" include direct and indirect references to community-engaged scholarship. While the document does not give the history of how the university made the decision to integrate language that seems relevant to civically engaged scholarship, it is specified that the document was approved by the University Council in 2004, and it has been revised several times. I am referencing the document as per revisions in the spring of 2014. Interestingly, while there is language relevant to civically engaged scholarship under the research/creative and the service sections, this is not the case for the teaching section. Four specific criteria seem relevant, under "Contributions to Research, Scholarship and Other Creative Activities":

1. Number 9: Description of outreach or other activities in which there was significant use of candidate's expertise (e.g. consultant, journal editor, reviewer for refereed journal, peer reviewer of grants, speaker, service to government agencies, professional and industrial associations, educational institutions).

2. Number 10: Description of new courses and/or programs developed, including service-learning and outreach courses at home or abroad, where research and new knowledge are integrated.
3. Number 14: Application of research scholarship in the field, including new applications developed and tested; new or enhanced systems and procedures demonstrated or evaluated for government agencies, professional and industrial associations, or educational institutions.
4. Number 17: Other evidence of impact on society of research scholarship and creative accomplishment. (p. 18)

The section "Contributions in Service to Society, the University and the Profession" includes the following definition of *serving society*, as well as specific examples: "Service to society refers to the function of applying academic expertise to the direct benefit of external audiences in support of unit and university missions. It can include applied research, service-based instruction, program and project management and technical assistance" (p. 18). In addition, it names the following five specific conditions that must be met for faculty work to count as service to society:

1. There is utilization of the faculty member's academic and professional expertise.
2. There is a direct application of knowledge to, and a substantive link with, significant human needs and societal problems, issues or concerns.
3. The ultimate purpose is for the public or common good.
4. New knowledge is generated for the discipline and/or the audience or clientele.
5. There is a clear relationship between the program/activities and an appropriate academic unit's mission. (p. 19)

It is very important to recognize, acknowledge, and celebrate the many higher education leaders and academics who have contributed to this movement, as well as their victories. Yet, it is equally important to recognize that this progress has been slow, as the opening of this article so clearly articulates (Warden, 2014):

> The number of academics who step outside the ivory tower to engage with the community is growing and universities are using a variety of ways to compensate them for doing so. But institutions that recognise and reward this effort are still very much a minority and the reasons why they find it hard to do are complex.

Warden illustrates this comment with findings from research performed by Clare Snyder-Hall, who works as an independent researcher in the United

States, and Lorlene Hoyt, who works for the Talloires Network. Warden reports that Snyder-Hall's research found that 22 of 40 academics she interviewed were institutionally rewarded, but that this happened only because they were able to integrate engagement activities into their scholarship or other institutional positions. This means that in the absence of institutionally established rewards, these academics were able to design their work in a way that included their civically engaged work.

To give an institutional perspective, I offer this excerpt from an interview with a USC senior administrator, specifically related to rewarding faculty for public and innovative scholarship:

> In terms of service-learning, it is an issue of the buy-in from faculty. People will say, "This is important." And then you say, "Will you participate or will you step forward?" And they say, "I'm so busy and my research . . . ." Particularly with research universities, and it's an easy way to say why things don't happen but it's the incentives for faculty. If the incentives are there people will get on board. I was talking to a chemistry professor this morning who was interested in doing more in terms of early years undergraduate teaching in STEM fields. He was talking about the rewards system and the truth is for young faculty who often have—well, I won't say they always have the most energy but they have innovative ideas. The reward systems run counter to what we're talking about if we're talking about innovative teaching and working with undergraduates because publications and research productivity and whatever the field is, is how they will be judged when they come up for tenure. And often the administration will make statements that teaching is on an equal footing with research. But by the time you come up for review in your department it's going to be your research work that is evaluated from the outside and usually the decisions are based on that. And so it can be difficult to get the momentum and the faculty that are pushing and that are actually willing to take part in some of these things. (Personal communication, November 8, 2016)

This faculty member also mentioned a number of very impressive public, innovative, and interdisciplinary teaching and research collaborations, but stated that these are mostly done by nontenure-track, often part-time, faculty and civic engagement staff. While many nontenure-track faculty and civic engagement staff perform important public engagement work, they tend to be limited as far as their power to influence institutional reward systems, or any type of culture change. This brings up another challenge in advancing this movement, which relates to something many of us have experienced on our campuses, with the decrease of tenured faculty and an increase in part-time faculty. While faculty may sometimes be judged for not using more of their collective civic agency to take action on creating institutional change, there are many institutional barriers to act, even when faculty are willing. For example, this senior USC faculty member conveys a sense of powerlessness, and what could easily be seen as a rationale for faculty working in silos, a situation very common in higher education.

> Well, I had hopes at one point of creating a center for civic engagement at USC . . . having links to people all over the university and outside the university. . . . When I came here it was highly decentralized. It was essentially a collection of professional schools with a very weak college [Dornsife College of Letters, Arts and Sciences]. And now they have strengthened the college a lot. A lot. But the professional schools are still there as powerful actors, so it is very hard to institutionalize anything university-wide here unless it comes from the provost, the president of the university and even then it is difficult to do. . . . So, I have decided just to work within this school and with people that I have some common ground with. (USC faculty member, personal communication, summer 2014)

In spite of these limitations, this faculty member is still able to engage on campus, locally, and internationally, but this type of scenario can be discouraging for faculty who are pursuing tenure and promotion, and who are overwhelmed by their relatively new jobs. Yet, as Clare Snyder-Hall's research mentioned by Warden (2014) found, many academics choose to engage their scholarship with external publics, because that gives meaning to their work. In many ways, their civically engaged scholarship transforms them professionally and personally. Likewise, many senior-level administrators, such as the well-known public work of former chancellor of Syracuse University Nancy Cantor (Cantor & Englot, 2015), have put their democratic values into practice. Although Cantor and Englot (2015) recognize that institutional reward systems for civically engaged scholarship are critical, they add that "it is also critical that we think more broadly about the culture of work in the academy—that is, about where and with whom and for what purposes we do this work, not to mention who we are as a community of scholars and students and professional staff" (p. 76). Thus, they argue that the creation of an ecosystem of whole communities is an essential foundation for public scholars.

Creating an ecosystem of whole communities based on updated information on who we are as university communities and especially who constitutes the majority of faculty these days is important. During my years at Occidental, as staff working with faculty, I focused on tenured and tenure-track faculty, coming from a perspective that they were the ones with the most direct personal and professional interest in transforming the culture of the college, and also the ones with the most long-term sustained power.

This made sense, because at least at the time, tenured and tenure-track faculty members were a substantial percentage of the total faculty body, and many of them have stayed there for 20 to 30 years. In contrast, at USC and at CSUDH, in my roles as postdoctoral fellow and tenure-track faculty, respectively, I learned that the number of tenured and tenure-track faculty has considerably decreased. I have since learned that this scenario has become common in many colleges and universities, where adjuncts and full-time lecturers have become the majority.

Adrianna Kezar and Daniel Maxey (2015) affirm that these changes have been in the making for decades. In their article, "Adapting by Design: Creating Faculty Roles and Defining Faculty Work to Ensure an Intentional Future for Colleges and Universities," Kezar and Maxey assert,

> Over the last 40 years, the traditional model of the academic profession full-time tenure-track professorships that focus on the triadic responsibilities of teaching, research, and service has been eroded by a rising trend toward greater contingency. This trend has broken those responsibilities apart, with faculty members increasingly finding themselves focusing primarily on either teaching or research and having tenuous connections to the academic community on their own campuses and to other scholars in their disciplines more broadly. Tenure-track jobs, which were once the most prevalent appointments on campuses, are being supplanted by an ever-rising number of full and part-time non-tenure-track faculty positions. These contingent appointments now make up approximately 70% of faculty positions responsible for providing instruction in the nonprofit higher education sector. (p .5)

The authors confirm what many of us academics know from experience: Faculty workload has increased, while support and resources have decreased. This, they find, has detrimental implications for student success and retention, and it also has implications for meeting the complex demands on higher education, as well as its public purpose. As a member of the CSUDH Academic Senate (2015–2017), I have been part of many discussions on this subject. Some such discussion, aided by organizing efforts from campus leadership for the California Faculty Association (statewide union for California state institutions), has led to institutional changes that have given adjunct faculty more of a role in faculty-related decision-making. This may well be a new and growing pattern in higher education, evolving from what Kezar and Maxey have documented.

It is clear, then, that for universities to realize their public, democratic mission, a myriad of financial, institutional, and societal challenges need to be recognized. It is equally clear that those who have been practicing civically engaged scholarship are finding their work transformational for themselves, for students, for institutions, and for communities. Many of these leaders are also aware that more need to join the movement. In this growing movement, reciprocity has become a significant part of the discourses about what constitutes successful, equitable partnerships with external communities, but this concept is also important in creating collaborations inside higher education institutions. Can reciprocity help us create the webs of relationships necessary to create a higher education culture that values and rewards this type of scholarship, thereby acting on this public, democratic mission?

Reciprocal and Transformational Civically Engaged Scholarship

The online English Oxford Living Dictionaries (2017) defines *reciprocity* as "the practice of exchanging things with others for mutual benefit, especially privileges granted by one country or organization to another." Mutuality is a concept widely used in the field of civic engagement as an essential component of partnerships between universities and communities, but it does not always include an understanding by both parties of what commodities they might possess that would be relevant to exchange with each other, for their mutual benefit. Discussion of mutuality in civic engagement literature too often comes from the perspective of civic engagement theorists and practitioners, and, for the most part, not from community partners' perspectives. An ideal definition of *mutuality* would imply equal benefits for all in a partnership; however, Clayton, Bringle, Senor, Huq, and Morrison (2010) offer a perspective in which only one party may benefit at least temporarily, possibly as an early stage in achieving mutuality.

The online English Oxford Living Dictionaries' (2017) definition of *reciprocity* also states that this definition is rooted in "French *réciprocité*, from *réciproque*, and in Latin *reciprocus* 'moving backward and forward.'" This Latin definition calls for a process, a back-and-forth between faculty and those with whom they partner. I resonate with the elements of mutuality and a process of back-and-forth, but I also know that operationalizing this definition can be a long and complicated endeavor. This is so to a large extent because reciprocity evolves based on context, and the interests, knowledge, and resources of those involved in the partnerships. Hence, reciprocity evolves in the relationality that is created by the back-and-forth between faculty and community partners. Equally important, this cocreative process involves issues of power and status and differences in cultures and reward systems and can be very labor intensive.

And yet when partners engage in an attempt to operationalize this full definition of *reciprocity*, this can be transformational for faculty and for community partners, as well as for students (and anyone else involved, as I illustrated in chapter 3). The back-and-forth element, then, implies an evolving relationship out of which all in the partnership get to know each other's interests, resources, and type of knowledge. This is what Castillo, Freer, Guillen, and Maeda (2015) demonstrate. To Castillo and her colleagues, reciprocity involves "developing ownership of the pedagogy with and by all the stakeholders of community-based learning and research—faculty students and community partners" (p. 290). Emphasizing the importance of faculty ownership and leadership in the success and sustainability of the CCBL (which Castillo directs), the authors add the following:

> This sense of ownership is developed by identifying and connecting to each group's and individual's motivation (in community organizing terms "self-interest") for utilizing or engaging with the pedagogy. All of the stakeholders are involved in the decision-making process when developing projects together. Each stakeholder defines what he or she wants out of a partnership in order to ensure that any work done together truly benefits all who are involved. Ensuring that each stakeholder is clear about what he or she hopes to gain through the partnership is foundational for developing long-term reciprocal relationships. (p. 290)

This statement comes from reflections from Castillo and three faculty members in politics, Spanish, and critical theory and social justice, about their work and journeys as their civically engaged scholarship continues to evolve.

Clayton and her colleagues further examine these and other aspects of good practice in service-learning and civic engagement and make a distinction between transformational and transactional relationships. They state that not all relationships need to be transformational.

> Transactional relationships and outcomes may be appropriate in some situations; movement toward mutual transformation may be desirable in other situations. What is needed is a means of making visible the full range of possibilities and distinguishing between actual and desired states, so that persons involved in any given relationship (and those who support them) can more effectively discuss, diagnose, and, as desired, deepen the quality of interactions. (2010, p. 8)

The authors recognized that while *reciprocity* is often used when the aim is to achieve mutuality, for there to be transformation for all in the partnership "a 'thicker' use of this term" is needed to acknowledge elements of power and ownership of products resulting from the relationship (p. 18). Building this type of relationship is likely to involve tension, disappointments, and power struggles, and the end result is not always as great as expected. What is certain is that a romantic notion of "helping" others, or feelings of altruism, although an element of many partnerships, is not effective as the main ingredient driving this cocreative, relationship-building process. Whether we all agree with the various levels of relationality, we can all agree that transformation, whether personal, professional, institutional, or community, does not come easily or quickly.

Although this discussion of reciprocity is mainly focused on faculty and their community partners, students are usually part of the equation, often as research assistants or in civically engaged classes, as I discussed in chapter 3. While there are many great examples of successful student reciprocal engagement with community partners, there are also instances in which, if not guided properly, student engagement can be damaging to them and to those with whom they engage. To this effect, Occidental professor Caroline Heldman (2011), writing about her civically engaged scholarship work in post-Katrina New Orleans, warns that "community-based learning placement that involves college students working with disadvantaged populations may involve students' enacting their privilege in ignorant and insensitive ways" (p. 33). It is therefore something faculty, students, and community partners must ideally discuss prior to or early in the partnership. As Eric Wat, a community partner for a class I taught at USC in 2012, put it, these types of conversations are more the exception than the norm, but without them, student placement can do more harm than good for the students and for the emerging partnership.

Operationalizing the Concept of Reciprocity

To add to the examples offered in chapter 3 from Occidental, I offer an international perspective through two interview excerpts from Maynooth University (conducted in 2010, compiled in 2016). The first is from a sociology professor, and the second is from a community partner with the adult and community education department. Maynooth's sociology professor began by describing a degree in her department called Politics and Active Citizenship:

> We look at power and politics from below, beyond the usual aspects of politics, and we look closely at the concept of active citizenship and social movements. The first semester students look at citizenship and how democracy works at the university. . . . They look at what happens on campus, in the classroom, and so on. The second semester they do experiential learning. [For example,] they might be working with a politician, they might be working with an NGO [non-governmental organization] . . . in Parliament; it has to be connected to power. (Personal communication, November 1, 2016)

She explained that she understands the difference between engaging students with community service to enhance their learning of academic subjects while exposing them to their role in society and doing this in reciprocity with community partners' interests. This is how she put it:

> At the end, they [students] write a paper on their reflections about the experience, but I am less concerned with their service to the organization than with their observation and learning about the dynamics of power. I don't want the students to be working in the back room, but I want them to be out where they can observe the dynamics of power, and I am not sure how much service [for the organization] they can do in that sense. (Personal communication, November 1, 2016)

Although this might seem to be an uneven partnership, such as the type previously mentioned by Clayton and colleagues where only one party benefits, this academic then described a different type of mutual benefit:

> What organizations [community partners] are saying, which I find very interesting, is that they are very conscious of the need for the university to grow civically minded students for the future . . . [and] having a role in this is a way of gaining something in the partnership. . . . They also recognize other ways in which they benefit from working with me as a *pracademic*, which means that you are very action research oriented, [with] a large ethos to your own work to be relevant. You take a piece of research and the organization finds it useful but it's done by the academic. This is different from participatory action research in that the community does not take part in doing the actual research. (Personal communication, November 1, 2016)

She explained that part of why she is able to build these partnerships is because she has brought the networks from her past work with NGOs (before becoming an academic) to her academic work. She spoke passionately about this, stating that "quite a large part of my commitment as an academic is to give time to doing research that enables community groups to be more effective; that's where the civic engagement comes from" (personal communication, November 1, 2016). A public scholar from USC's American studies and ethnicity department and another from the history department shared a very similar definition of *mutuality* with their community partners. What is important to note here is that in all cases, according to the academics, there was a mutual understanding of the concept of mutuality, and this in itself was an important element of cocreating the partnerships.

The director of a community organization who partners with Maynooth's adult and community education department shared a different perspective regarding how she and those in her community benefit from the partnership. She shared that her organization provides a site where the adult and community education department offers courses leading to certificates related to mental health:

> I am happy with the partnership, especially with the skills that community residents are gaining through the Psychology Programme. After the students complete a year-long programme on psychology, some of them go on to further their education, others use what they learn personally or with their families, and others use it in their professional work. (Personal communication, fall semester, 2010).

Academics from the adult and community education department expressed that being able to offer their programs in community settings is closely connected to their mission of contributing to community and societal change. By doing this, they and the university also benefit from revenue generated by registered students. This notion of mutual benefit is shared by the community partner cited previously, who elaborated on her vision of how this could be improved:

> [For example,] universities could gather people in various communities and get feedback for what course offerings are relevant regarding current issues, especially in fields like psychology and social work. University students do not graduate with the skills to deal with serious issues. This worries me because there is a high rate of sexual abuse, and most social workers lack awareness and the skills to effectively respond to this when they graduate. The university would benefit from community feedback financially [because] this could increase interest in enrolling in the university. I believe any method of education needs to be based on feedback. (Phone interview, fall semester, 2010)

This community partner viewed this role of the university as part of its democratic mission and commented that

> because democracy should be more transparent, less greedy, more spiritual, and more respectful of everyone in society, values and ethics need to be part of the curriculum for all disciplines, including law and business, not just English literature, for instance, where values are naturally part of the curriculum.

A USC policy academic shared what I would view as an example of a reciprocal partnership that fulfills all elements of mutual benefit and the process of back-and-forth described by the Oxford Dictionary, and the "thickness" mentioned by Clayton and colleagues (2010). This USC academic also discusses the tensions inherited in this type of relationship building, such as issues of power and status between the academic and the institution he represents, and the community partner and the organization and community she represents. An important foundation for this relationship is that it had existed for over 20 years as of the spring semester of 2013, when I conducted this interview. I will refer to the community partner as L. Following is the story this academic told me:

> In 1998, L. had created a really interesting group of people that she put together because she felt that the health disparities between African Americans and White Americans seemed to be increasing when it should be declining. So they went out and got a planning grant from the Centers for Disease Control in a program that CDC had just set up called The Racial and Ethnic Approaches to Community Health Reach. And she came to me in late 1999, so we had this year to prove to the federal government that we should get funding. At the time I taught a studio in a graduate program in urban planning and, with these five intrepid students who thought I was crazy because in 2000, planners didn't do food . . . and so essentially, we did an environmental scan of South Los Angeles, around physical activity and food systems. We actually were able to give them a 50-page report that outlined the areas of concern, highlighted the extraordinary fast-food proliferation in South LA. Talked about [lack of] parks, private services like recreation centers or gyms, or anything like that. We included that, as part of their application for $3 million over five years, to try and diminish the disparities of African Americans in South LA around cardiovascular disease and diabetes. They then got the grant. And in some weird odd circumstance, L. asked me to help her for a year, to think about how to do assessments around food and physical activity, and 13 years later [2013, at the time of this interview], we are still doing them. Our partnership has often generated public attention from media, but we've always had a very strong belief that the community should speak for the community. So one of the things now that [the community partnering organization] has gotten mature enough, a year and a half ago, they started a program to build community research capacity. So what it's about is, we've been doing surveys since 2000, and we've had dozens if not hundreds of people do surveys for [the organization and for USC]. We have always had as part of our training that we want to leave you with the power, that if somebody comes to your door and says I want to do a survey with you, you can do it yourself and you can ask the right questions about what the heck are you going to do with the results? And is this for the community? Or are you just taking from the community? That's

always been one of our messages, but we always felt that it was haphaz-
ard. What we hope is eventually we'll have enough people so when [for
example] another university comes to South LA, and says [they're] going
to do surveys, community organizations can say, "We got surveyors for
you." And that changes the power dynamic. So when we did an article on
grocery stores in 2004, that was our second or third article we were able
to produce on the project. And it was really a big deal, it sort of amped
everything up, and L. sat down with me, and said, "We have to figure out
a publication protocol where we ensure you guys don't just go do this,
where we're involved." And it is the kind of thing we have done all the
way through, we have always thought of it as a reciprocal relationship
that should build both sides. There has to be a balance of power. You have
to have that dynamic, or you're not going to make the progress you want
to make. You're going to get stuck with one side or the other, unhappy,
feeling left out of the conversation and it could be either side. (Personal
communication [to edit 2013 interview], November 8, 2016)

In the process described here, both parties in the partnership evolved
together, had their ups and downs, and through it built the "thickness" in the
relationship that allowed them to discuss moments of tension, discuss power
and status differentials, produce socially and academically useful knowledge,
and even publish together. Although there may be many partnerships that
embody these and other elements of an ideal level of reciprocity, details of
what this looks like are not often found in the literature.

In addition, the academic brought up some of the dynamics that are also
rarely found in the literature, and that can get in the way of creating the type
of partnership he and L. were able to build:

I think it's difficult for lots of researchers who are normally very much
in control. And it's difficult for community-based organizations because
they're very fragile, and the leadership has to be strong. And so there are
other examples around town where you would imagine they would have
much stronger relationships with researchers than they do. Not to name
anybody, but there's a couple I can name off the top of my head, and I'm
sure you can too, who are really good, very powerful organizations that
aren't doing really great research, and should be, you would think. But they
have never found the partner that they need, or they're unwilling to work
with the partner. (Personal communication, 2013)

This story is a great example of the extent to which USC could effect change
with its surrounding communities, if this type of long-term engagement were
to be institutionalized within the reward system. Why is this not the case?

A Community Partner's Summary: The Market, Faculty Rewards, and Reciprocity

A story from Eric Wat, the USC community partner mentioned earlier in this chapter, summarized the three main topics discussed in this chapter—namely, the influence of the market in higher education and other types of institutions; the challenges of the current status of faculty rewards; and the complexity of building partnerships that are reciprocal for the partner, the academic, and the students. Wat has a background in higher education as an administrator and part-time faculty, and therefore his perspective is relevant to higher education and to community partners. He was my community partner for an internship-based CBL class I taught in USC's American studies and ethnicity department, called Leadership in the Community. At first, he was reluctant to join the partnership because my class was undergraduate level, and he prefers to work with graduate students. He agreed to host one of my students because I explained that I would be involved in the process with him and with the student throughout the semester. A theme that runs throughout the story is the important role relationships play in building meaningful partnerships that, on the one hand, benefit all parties and, on the other, do not cause hardship. He addresses a reality that affects many who practice civically engaged teaching and research, and he powerfully speaks to the pros and cons of institutionalizing this type of teaching and research as a vehicle to create culture change in higher education.

My first exposure to community engagement with a university setting was through UCLA. I was working at the Asian American Studies Center between 1994 and 1997. Because it's an ethnic studies center, it has a very explicit mission in terms of community engagement. At that time, the point of having ethnic studies was not only training people in the university system but also taking that knowledge out in the community and actually training community members who don't have access to higher education. It's that kind of two-way street that's missing even in ethnic studies now. I'm not as close to it as before, but I don't hear people talking about "Let's bring this class out into the community." We were opening classes to the community, doing joint events in the community and on campus. So there was a lot more engagement. I have to say, I admire people who work in the university system because I know there are a lot of limitations. There are so many demands placed on faculty, especially junior faculty of color, because there is always pressure to get published, to get tenure, so that you have stability. So I kind of appreciate [the way] you talk about community engagement. What I got from it is that it's not only about improving and changing the community but it is also about changing the university. I was at UCLA at a time when ethnic studies was still growing in the 1990s and becoming a little more mainstream. I remember when a faculty member who was very active in the community got a tenure-track position and his colleagues told the community, "Leave him alone for a couple of years. Let him get published." At UCLA one of my responsibilities was to coordinate internships within the class setting. Because professors could not pay students, we thought what if we give students class credit. But at the same time, there are all these issues. It's really hard to do a really meaningful internship, as we all know, because students have a really limited time. I think especially now more than 20 years ago, people are not really staying in college for five years anymore because they can't afford to. They need to get out fast because higher education is so unaffordable. They can't really explore as much as they used to, like with my generation, we would say, "Oh, let's stay another quarter because I want to take these classes." I don't think that happens anymore. And in addition, they're working already, a lot of students. I taught at California State University and I had students who came to evening class after working eight hours somewhere, and they're tired. So I think our idea of community engagement is very challenging. . . . You have the university structure, which places a lot of demands on faculty, you have an economic system that places a lot of demand on the students, and people want to do community engagement but there are all of these limitations. Some faculty say, "If you do this, we'll count it toward something in the university," but no one is really addressing the fact that I, at a community site, can't really have a meaningful relationship with the student if there are all these things pulling her away. . . . Faculty has to be involved. I think the thing that really made Rosemary [a student from my class] work, and I think that's the first time that I really took an undergrad intern . . . it was because there was faculty involvement, and there were other people who were making sense of that relationship on my staff. It is not that I don't want to have undergraduate interns, but I know how hard it is to find a meaningful experience with them and I don't want to do a half-assed job. So community engagement is tricky. I think when you're a grad student you have a little bit more support. We have graduate interns for three months in the summer, for 30 hours a week. We pay them, not well, but we pay them and we get to be in the project together, they get to see how it works on a day-to-day basis, and we see that it's a pipeline. Some of them come back as staff, and want to do this more. It's about relationship building. Regarding your question on institutionalizing civic engagement [in the curriculum], my gut reaction is, to have any sustainability it's always better to be institutionalized. But, in that formula, the individual is also very key. So I'm thinking about a lot of the stuff that I used to do at UCLA that is no longer there, even though it was institutionalized. So sometimes institutionalization might mean a little more stability, but sometimes maybe not. But at least if it's institutionalized, then you have the structure there that you can improve on. Or maybe I'm just being too cynical that if you have new people coming in, they're not going to share your same vision, and they're going to bastardize the program.

But, yeah, I think institutionalization is important. The DNA is the reward system. You can do this, but you still have to do all your other stuff too. You still have to join committees, you still want to get published, you still have to get blah, blah, blah . . . and we will put you in our newsletter, and we will talk about community engagement and talk about how integrated USC is with the neighborhoods. So institutionalization is possible to get some resources but it just takes a lot of resources. I think we need really good matchmakers between faculty and community-based organizations. These matchmakers have to have one foot in the community and one foot within academia and both very solid, because you need the relationship with the community organization and you need the relationship with the faculty. There are so many differences. I think there's such a huge learning curve for community folks around the reward system and how to work it, I think without feeling they're taking things too personally. I don't take it personally when faculty don't call me back, because I know . . . and you have a different kind of reward system in the nonprofit sector, too. I have seen so many organizations driven by economics more and more, and the foundations tell them to. So you do it if it pays. It's kind of sad, it's the business model. You do it, and you try to find a way to make it pay. So that takes investment, it takes relationship building. . . . Foundations want results right away. I should know, I'm steeped in this world, trying to tell foundations, "Hey, you can't give $50,000 and expect organizations to change the world," but they know there are other people that will do it for less. (E. Wat, personal communication, November 1, 2016)

What do we learn from Wat's account here? His comprehensive take on the various angles involved in the creation of partnerships that benefit all stakeholders is a sobering one. His perspective is informative and powerful, in that he describes aspects not often discussed, such as the business model utilized in the nonprofit and in the philanthropy sectors and his experience as an organization with a clear vision, purpose, and plan for hosting graduate students. In a sense, Wat's analysis resonates with Saltmarsh and Hartley's (2012) assertion that civic engagement has fallen short of its originally intended, democratic purpose, and it resonates with the relationality and the justice and action aspects of community organizing. Wat's reflections make me think of the long-term vision and mission of the type of societal and culture change we want to help create, and the relationships to do this collectively and across sectors.

The Benefits of Building Long-Term Relationships

I want to emphasize here the long-term, detailed, slow, and intentional process of building long-term, public relationships—that is, the type of relationships that are based on respect and accountability, to distinguish from private relationships, which are often based on intimacy, such as family and close friends. I discuss this in more detail in chapter 2. It is also important to note that in building this web of public relationships we must be intentional about cultivating and sustaining such relationships even if our jobs and institutions change. In this regard, my research at Maynooth had a relational foundation based on people I met during my first two trips to Ireland in 2005 and 2006, when I was invited to present at two conferences about my work at Occidental. These individuals then credentialed me to meet others who participated in my research. Without this relational foundation, I doubt I would have been able to gain the trust of the many civic, business, and academic leaders who participated in my research or a sense that the information they shared with me was true. Similarly, many of the civic, business, and academic leaders I interviewed through my USC research came from many years, one or two decades in many cases, of networking at various levels. The stories I tell about Occidental in chapter 3 came from long-term relationships I built during my tenure as an administrator at that institution, some of whom I met to reflect about our past work together in 2013, two years after I left the college.

I brought many of my Occidental and USC relationships with me to my faculty job at CSUDH, and, building from past projects, we together created new opportunities to partner through my classes and, in some cases, through field placements for our Master of Social Work students. Many of my relationships at the national level built through my work at Occidental have also been important in my work with IA and in my collaborations with Kettering. Ledwith and Springett (2010) also highlight the long-term relational aspect of participatory practice, specifically as they mention their long-term dialogical relationship of 17 years, prior to writing their book.

In line with this, the lessons I learned from Occidental, Maynooth, USC, and IA, as well as the partnerships I have built in those contexts, carried over to my tenure-track faculty position at CSUDH, in the Master of Social Work program. As it turns out, the challenges of civically engaged academics I have known thus far by working closely with and interviewing faculty have become my own. That is, I am faced with juggling the demands of teaching, research, and service, all while learning about this new institution, and a completely different job, all while becoming a civically engaged scholar.

And yet, there is privilege in being tenure-track faculty, such as flexibility of schedule (outside of scheduled courses) and a new level of status and recognition, even as an untenured faculty, which I did not anticipate. I sense this when interacting with faculty colleagues, with administrators, with students, with community partners, and even with friends and family. This flexibility and new status give me a different and welcomed arena from which to organize, but also a firsthand experience of what other faculty I have worked with in past roles have been dealing with all along. This new role and the status that comes with it credentialed me, for instance, to start a research-in-action project at CSUDH in 2015, only a year after I was hired. In brief, this project aims to explore questions related to the extent to which faculty from disciplines that have a mandate to be civically engaged, such as nursing, occupational therapy, labor studies, community sciences, and social work, are interested in using community organizing through their civically engaged scholarship.

With this new perspective on civically engaged scholarship, I remain committed to creating spaces where individual civic agency can be turned into collective civic agency, so that higher education institutions can live up to their public, democratic mission.

5

CONCLUDING POINTS AND
FINAL REFLECTIONS

I start this closing chapter with a strong conviction that community organizing can offer an approach to create the culture change in higher education that is essential for reciprocal, transformational, cocreated campus-community engagement. I argue that for this type of engagement to occur, faculty must enact their individual civic agency and turn this into collective, collaborative civic agency with other faculty colleagues, with their students, and with those with whom they partner in external communities. When faculty engage in this type of collective agency, this process can lead to creating change within higher education institutions, and it can also lead to transforming themselves, their students, and their community partners. I know this because I have been part of such organizing efforts for over a decade.

While specific organizing processes and contexts vary, four community organizing practices I learned through 10 years of organizing with the IAF have been integrated in all these contexts. These practices are one-to-one meetings, creating a collective of leaders, analyzing power dynamics, and ongoing critical reflection. These four practices are part of a process that can lead to strategic action on issues based on self, collective, institutional, and community interests of those involved. The various contexts in which I have used these practices are Occidental College in Los Angeles, Maynooth University in Ireland, USC in Los Angeles, IA, and CSUDH in Carson (in the Los Angeles metropolitan area).

Many Occidental faculty members were already engaged with off-campus community partners when the CCBL was created in 2011, but through this community organizing approach to civic engagement they were able to turn their individual civic engagement into collective civic engagement. In doing so, they transformed the culture of the institution from one that was focused on student community service to one with a primary focus on reciprocal, civically engaged scholarship. They did this through a slow yet strategic relational process on and off campus. This new culture fostered the creation of many reciprocal campus-community partnerships across the disciplines; it made it possible for civically engaged scholarship to count for tenure and promotion; and it allowed for the creation of a program through which students were paid to assist faculty with CBL and CBR, while developing their collective civic engagement skills. In this newly created culture, we organized a network of campus and off-campus partners in northeast Los Angeles, with the purpose of creating a college-going culture in the region.

At Maynooth University in Ireland, I was able to integrate community organizing through my doctoral research, as I explored, along with many faculty and administrators, their interest in institutionalizing civically engaged scholarship. Through this project, a collaborative of faculty was created that continued after the culmination of my research, and through which faculty organized a campus-wide gathering where they explored, with a newly hired president, possibilities for institutionalizing civic engagement. Thus, civically engaged faculty engaged in collective civic agency. I did a similar research project through a postdoctoral fellowship at USC, which led to various gatherings of faculty and administrators, and one final gathering that included faculty and community leaders. In these gatherings, participants discussed possible initiatives to officially and intentionally institutionalize civic engagement in the curriculum. I want to emphasize that while these two research projects did not lead to the level of transformation observed at Occidental, the fact that even in my short-term and less institutionalized roles as doctoral student and postdoctoral fellow I was able to create such collaboratives signals the potential community organizing has to create culture change and collaborative civic engagement.

My work with IA has focused on efforts that explore and foster civically engaged scholarship at a local, regional, and national level through community organizing. Through my collaborations with IA I have also received support from the Kettering Foundation with my postdoctoral research, as well as with civically engaged scholarship research at CSUDH, in my role as tenure-track faculty in the Master of Social Work program. In this capacity, in 2015 I began a research-in-action project with faculty from disciplines that have a mandate to be civically engaged, to explore integrating community organizing in their civically engaged scholarship. Included in this project were faculty from nursing, occupational therapy, peace and conflict resolution, labor studies, community science, and social work.

Of the four organizing practices I have used in my work in higher education, I consider one-to-one meetings the most important, particularly because of their potential to learn about people's self-interest and to learn whether and how these interests can lead to building collective leadership. The best way to learn about others' self-interest, as well as our own, is through exchanging stories about things that really matter to us, and that can therefore move us to take action on issues that affect us and our loved ones. These stories relate to our narrative, to who we are and where we come from, as well as our hopes and aspirations for the future. Our narratives are important, and sharing them with others can be transformational and grounding; most importantly, it can help us create a collective narrative that counters the current dominant narrative created and sustained by those with power and resources. Understanding and sharing our narratives can be a very powerful way of agitating us, by exposing us to experiences different from ours and, in this process, challenging previous beliefs and assumptions. Sharing narratives can therefore build solidarity in action to create change that affects us and others with whom we are engaged.

Although civically engaged scholarship has proliferated in the United States and in many other countries, this has not led to creating a predominant culture in higher education where creating reciprocal campus-community partnerships is valued, supported, and rewarded. There are examples of campuses where this has taken place at various levels, but this is not always predominant as an institutional culture. I am aware that the reasons for this are multilayered, and therefore they are complex. Yet there is enough evidence that the success of pro-market forces and policies worldwide in creating a culture that values individualism and profit making has had a major influence in the emergence of the current business model under which many higher education institutions and other public organizations currently operate. Under this model, spaces where collaborative civically engaged scholarship can flourish are rare.

This success of the market did not happen overnight, as documented by many scholars who have traced its development to at least four decades back (Brown, 2005; Newfield, 2011). Thus, this is a movement that has been intentionally organized. This means that its success did not happen by chance, or by wishful thinking. Recognizing and understanding this current reality is essential in visioning the type of counterculture we aim to create, as well as the specific strategies to do so in higher education and in society at large.

This current reality has many layers, including the fact that different institutions, disciplines, scholars, and community partners have different notions of what higher education's public mission and purposes are and should be. For instance, senior administration in many colleges and universities often view their institutional public mission as engaging with off-campus partners that can offer internships for students and/or funds for university initiatives. Disciplines such as social work and education often view their public purpose through the work students do through field placement. Community partners often view colleges and universities as partners in improving socioeconomic conditions of areas surrounding these higher education institutions. Another important layer of this reality is the fact that there are power dynamics and agendas among disciplinary fields often influenced by funders that shape research agendas, methods, incentives, and priorities.

These and many other aspects of our reality, however, are rarely part of discourses and initiatives related to creating reciprocal, civically engaged scholarship. Instead, at the great majority of gatherings where civically engaged scholarship is discussed, the conversations often turn into complaints about senior administration; their managerial, business models; and how these models and practices take resources and power away from faculty. Administrators, too, often complain about faculty being happier in their silos than participating in institutional and community projects. Many stakeholders outside of academia, such as civic, government, and business leaders, criticize colleges and universities for what they perceive to be detachment from social problems. This is all part of the dominant culture that does not offer incentives and spaces for collaborative work where the well-being of the collective is as important as that of the individual.

As I have experienced it, many academics, students, administrators, and community partners are open to being part of collective efforts that change the culture of the places where they work. I have met them in all the contexts in which I have worked, as they have engaged with me in my organizing efforts. In this organizing process we have witnessed significant transformation of our students, our institutions, our communities, and ourselves. My hope is that more such spaces can be created, and that they lead to building a movement that enhances democratic values and practices.

Building such a movement, similar to neoliberalism, will not happen overnight, or by chance, or by wishful thinking. Relatedly, isolated, spontaneous marches and demonstrations are also not effective for long-term change, although they can sometimes accomplish short-term victories. This is one difference between activism and organizing. As defined by Mark Rudd (2013), *activism* is mainly about self-expression, and *organizing* is about movement building. To be clear, movement building does not require that we all become community organizers, but it does require that we patiently and strategically build leadership collectives where we can together learn and practice the political and relational skills that are part of public life. This can start with reflecting on our own individual narratives, so that we can understand our purpose, as we learn and commit to acting on the rights and responsibilities that we have inherited, to preserve and improve our world.

This practice has been common in traditions of some Native American nations, as they gather to solve social problems and engage in reflections about their ancestors seven generations past, and about imagining the world they can help create seven generations forward. I learned a similar practice through my IAF organizing, where we engaged in individual and collective reflections about our narratives. With time, I came to realize that in order to be effective in building collectives of leaders I needed to be grounded in my own narrative—the origin of my organizing work to create change in the world. Only then was I able to help others act on their own stories. We can start this movement building one one-to-one meeting at a time, one leadership collective at a time, in one institution at a time, and in one community at a time.

AFTERWORD

With the publication of this work, Maria Avila joins a small but growing number of authors shedding new light on the role that colleges and universities have played—and play today—in American society. One of those authors, Kenneth H. Wheeler (2011), published *Cultivating Regionalism: Higher Education and the Making of the American Midwest*. Another, Adrianna Kezar (2012), collected a book of incisive essays in her book *Embracing Non-tenure Track Faculty*. In addition, Harry Boyte (2017) and others have written extensively about this topic.

In the current climate, the story told by Wheeler (2011) is largely forgotten. He describes the creation and growth of a generation of small colleges, started by religious denominations, throughout the Midwest, in the 1830s, 1840s, and 1850s. These colleges were deeply engaged in the public life of the nation—many of them strongly abolitionist and practitioners of open admission and equal rights for women. At the same time, these schools were profoundly pragmatic and innovative as centers of learning and experimentation in agriculture and the sciences.

The colleges and universities described by Adrianna Kezar and Maria Avila have continued the tradition of complex connection to the economic life of their communities and the nation, but have, for the most part, lost the depth and breadth of civic engagement. And, in recent decades, the market has increasingly dominated the mission and culture of higher education. Schools now compete for gifts and grants from major corporations—in part because of a sharp and accelerating decline in public support from local and federal sources and in part because of the way neoliberal thinking has permeated every corner of American life, including its higher education institutions.

Maria Avila has spent the past 17 years navigating these currents in several college and university contexts. She states in chapter 1 that "civically engaged scholarship . . . is not generally supported, valued or rewarded" (p. 2). And she asserts that "recovering this historical democratic, public mission of higher education" (p. 10) is the goal of her fine book.

She applies the lessons and universals she learned as 1 of 13 children raised by her parents in Mexico; as a 17-year-old factory worker denied bathroom breaks and medical attention; as a full-time organizer in the IAF, the network that I codirect with Ernesto Cortes Jr.; and as a grad student and tenure-track faculty member to the challenge of recovering higher education's public mission. Her personal story is, in and of itself, extraordinary. And, if she decides to write another book, I hope that she delves into the various chapters of her life in more detail.

Her description of the four practices of organizing—a process of individual meetings, building a team of talented leaders, analyzing and using power effectively, and being willing to engage in in-depth reflection and evaluation—is key to her public life, her approach to her work, and to this book.

She leads us through a series of experiences in a number of college and university settings, as she applies those practices in her daily life. In doing so, she conveys both the possibilities and opportunities that emerge when someone applies these practices with skill and patience, but she also communicates the obstacles and setbacks that occur. She is not trying to tell the reader what to do. She is not straining to sell the reader a rosy picture of this effort. Instead, she shows what the work of organizing, in the context of higher education, looks like when it is done with professionalism on a day-to-day basis, over many years.

And she is frank about the very real power dynamics that make this work challenging. In the world of higher education, civic engagement often means channeling students to short-term service projects. Many of these efforts are well intentioned, but they often lack any real feel for the community partners involved. And they almost never lead to the kind of CBL and CBR that Maria Avila describes in her chapter of her time at Occidental.

I saw this firsthand several years ago when I was asked to speak to the civic engagement department at an Ivy League university. I was shocked to see that there were 17 full-time staff people in the department and asked them, at the start, what they did. As they did the rounds, it became clear that their primary function was to facilitate very limited service work by a small number of students—renting cars so the students could drive the 10 miles to the impoverished area where the projects were located, for instance. Their work might help a few local residents, but it would do nothing to engage, at any meaningful level, the long-term leaders of the community or the enormous resources and talent of the university.

This is a far cry from the small Midwestern colleges that challenged slavery and sexism in the mid-1800s in America. And that gap will be closed only by people—like Maria Avila—who understand the needs and gifts of local community residents and leaders, who are clearheaded in their analysis of the power and potential of colleges and universities, and who are using their time and their energy to bring those two worlds more closely and meaningfully in relationship.

Michael Gecan
Codirector of the Industrial Areas Foundation

Community Organizing's Similarities With Participatory Action Research

*P*articipatory action research (PAR) is one of many terms that relate to research that is connected to community relevance. Other terms include *action research, community-based research, emancipatory research,* and *community-based participatory research* (Minkler & Wallerstein, 2011; Munck, McIlrath, Hall, & Tandon, 2014; Strand, Marullo, Cutforth, Stoecker, & Donohue, 2003). As Munck and colleagues (2014) explain, what these concepts have in common is that the divide that commonly exists between academic researchers and community practitioners gets blurred. That is, the aim of this type of research is to, at best, involve those in communities where research is conducted to be coresearchers, and at a minimum to have input in what is to be researched. Given this brief definition, it is important to note some of the similarities among community organizing, PAR, and other research modalities that focus on creating social change and that value local knowledge.

I discovered PAR during my doctoral studies at Maynooth University while explaining the community organizing practices I had used to create the civic engagement model at Occidental to my academic supervisors, Anne Ryan and Brid Connolly, in the adult and community education department. In this conversation, we arrived at the conclusion that these organizing practices were similar to PAR, and that this similarly could aid as a theoretical framework for my research. Following are some of the main similarities that I have observed in my work as an academic where I combine the two modalities as relevant:

- Community organizing methods include one-to-one, relational meetings to learn about issues that affect community residents. One-to-one meetings are primarily focused on stories, rather than on superficial information. This organizing practice compares to PAR's in-depth narrative interviews, which are also relational and conversational. These interviews aim at learning about whether and to what extent the issues the researcher is exploring could be of interest to community residents affected by the research project.

- Community organizing involves those living and working in communities where the organizing is taking place, in the organizing process. PAR is also collaborative and participatory between researchers and community residents.
- Both community organizing and PAR aim to create long-term, sustainable social and culture change, through the creation of collaborative leadership collectives led by community organizers/researchers.
- Both methodologies are fluid and iterative. That is, often parts of the purpose of the research, as well as of the organizing goals, change based on interests and skills of those who become part of the collaborative leadership collectives.

In the context of these similarities, I now realize that I was a PAR researcher when I was an IAF organizer, and that I am an organizer now as an academic researcher.

GLOSSARY

Broad-based organizing
"A 'relational' and 'institutional' approach to social change that relies on the local knowledge of ordinary citizens to drive policy change and craft solutions to some of our most vexing social problems" (Amos Institute of Public Life, 2017).

California State University, Dominguez Hills (CSUDH)
CSUDH is one of 23 state universities in California, and it is located in Carson, which is within the Los Angeles metropolitan area.

Center for Community-Based Learning (CCBL) at Occidental College
The CCBL's mission is to institutionalize curriculum-based civic engagement.

Civically engaged scholarship
Partnerships between civically engaged faculty and their community partners through teaching and research.

Civic engagement
Partnerships between higher education institutions and community groups/organizations.

Community-based learning (CBL)
Instruction that combines classroom instruction with community projects.

Community-based research (CBR)
Research conducted by academic researchers and their community partners.

Community partners
Off-campus stakeholders with whom higher education institutions partner, usually through curricular or extracurricular projects.

Education in Action (EIA)
A program of the CCBL at Occidental, which hires students to assist civically engaged faculty.

Imagining America (IA)
A consortium of over 100 higher education institutions engaged with off-campus partners, primarily focused on the arts, humanities, and design.

Industrial Areas Foundation (IAF)
An international community organizing network founded in 1940 by Saul D. Alinsky.

Maynooth
Maynooth University, or the city of Maynooth, in County Kildare, Ireland.

Nongovernmental organizations (NGOs)
NGOs are not-for-profit organizations.

Northeast Education Strategy Group (NESG)
A regional network of educators in northeast Los Angeles, founded by the CCBL at Occidental College.

One LA-IAF
The IAF organization in the Los Angeles metropolitan area.

Partnerships to Uplift Communities (PUC) schools
A group of charter schools in northeast Los Angeles and East San Fernando Valley.

The Research University Civic Engagement Network (TRUCEN)
Advances civic engagement and scholarship within research universities.

Service-learning
Similar to CBL, this is instruction that combines classroom instruction with community projects.

University of Southern California (USC)
USC is a private, research 1 university in Los Angeles, California.

Alinsky, S. D. (1969). *Reveille for radicals.* New York, NY: Vintage Books.

Alinsky, S. D. (1971). *Rules for radicals: A practical primer for realistic radicals.* New York, NY: Random House.

Amos Institute of Public Life. (2017). *What is broad-based organizing? How is it different from other forms of social change?* Retrieved from http://amosipl.org/what-is-broad-based-community-organizing-how-is-it-different-from-other-forms-of-social-change/

Avila, M. (2010). Community organizing practices in academia: A model, and stories of partnerships. *Journal of Higher Education Outreach and Engagement, 14*(2), 37.

Benson, L., Harkavy, I., & Puckett, J. (2007). *Dewey's dream: Universities and democracies in an age of education reform.* Philadelphia, PA: Temple University Press.

Berger, D., Boudin, C., & Farrow, K. (2005). *Letters from young activists: Today's rebels speak out.* New York, NY: Nation Books. Also available at http://www.thenorthstar.info/?p=9474

Borja, R. (2012, Summer). Engaged and infused. *Occidental Magazine.* Retrieved from http://www.oxy.edu/magazine/summer-2012/engaged-infused

Boyer, E. L. (1990). *Scholarship reconsidered: Priorities of the professoriate.* Princeton, NJ: Carnegie Foundation for the Advancement of Teaching.

Boyer, E. L. (1996). The scholarship of engagement. *Journal of Public Service and Outreach, 1*(1), 11–20.

Boyte, H. C. (2004). *Everyday politics: Reconnecting citizens and public life.* Philadelphia: University of Pennsylvania Press.

Boyte, H. C. (2009). *Civic agency and the cult of the expert.* Dayton, OH: The Kettering Foundation.

Boyte, H. C. (2013). *Reinventing citizenship as public work: Citizen-centered democracy and the empowerment gap.* Dayton, OH: The Kettering Foundation.

Boyte, H. C. (2017, April). *Citizen politics and schools as civic centers: Will democracy survive big data and artificial intelligence?* John Dewey Society Lecture in San Antonio, TX. Retrieved from https://www.academia.edu/32440405/Boyte_Citizen_Politics_and_Schools_as_Civic_Centers_Draft_April_15_2017.docx

Brown, W. (2005). *Edgework: Critical essays on knowledge and politics.* Princeton, NJ: Princeton University Press.

Campus Compact. (2016a). *Mission and vision.* Retrieved from http://compact.org/who-we-are/mission-and-vision.

Campus Compact. (2016b). *TRUCEN.* Retrieved from http://compact.org/initiatives/trucen

Cantor, N. (2012, May 23). *The public mission of higher education: Barn raisings a century later.* Invited keynote address delivered at the University of Wisconsin-Madison Teaching & Learning Symposium, Advancing the Year of the Wisconsin Idea.

Cantor, N., & Englot, P. (2015). Reinventing scholar-educators as citizens and public workers. In H. C. Boyte (Ed.), *Democracy's education: Public work, citizenship, & the future of colleges and universities* (pp. 75–79). Nashville, TN: Vanderbilt University Press.

Castillo, C., Freer, R., Guillen, F., & Maeda, D. (2015). Faculty development and ownership of community-engaged teaching and learning. In N. W. Sobania (Ed.), *Putting the local in the global education: Models for transformative learning through domestic off-campus programs* (pp. 288–297). Sterling, VA: Stylus.

Chambers, E. T. (2003). *Roots for radicals: Organizing for power, action, and justice.* New York, NY: Bloomsbury.

Chin, E. J., & Núñez, M. (2006). Fostering a community-based learning culture: A model for success and institutional barriers. *North American Dialogue, 9*(1). Retrieved from http://works.bepress.com/elizabeth_chin/3/

Clayton, P. H., Bringle, R. G., Senor, B., Huq, J., & Morrison, M. (2010, Spring). Differentiating and assessing relationships in service-learning and civic engagement: Exploitative, transactional, or transformational. *Michigan Journal of Community Service Learning,* 5–22.

Colby, A., Ehrlich, T., with Beaumont, E., Rosner, J., & Stephens, J. (2000). Higher education and the development of civic responsibility. In T. Ehrlich (Ed.), *Civic responsibility and higher education* (pp. xxi–xliii). Phoenix, AZ: Oryx Press.

Cress, C. M., & Donahue, D. M. (2011). *Democratic dilemmas of teaching service-learning: Curricular strategies for success.* Sterling, VA: Stylus.

Dewey, J. (1937, May). Education and social change. *Social Frontier, 3,* 235–238.

Driscoll, A., & Lynton, E. (1999). *Making outreach visible: A guide to documenting professional service and outreach.* Washington, DC: American Association for Higher Education.

Duggan, L. (2007). Neoliberalism. In B. Burgett & G. Hendler (Eds.), *Keywords for American cultural studies* (p. 181). New York, NY: NYU Press.

Ehrlich, T. (2000). *Civic responsibility and higher education.* Phoenix, AZ: Oryx Press.

Ellison, J., & Eatman, T. (2008). *Scholarship in public: Knowledge creation and tenure policy in the engaged university: A resource on promotion and tenure in the arts, humanities, and design.* Retrieved from http://www.imaginingamerica.org/

Fear, F. A., Rosaen, C. L., Bawden, R. J., & Foster-Fishman, P. G. (2006). *Coming to critical engagement: An autoethnographic exploration.* Lanham, MD: University Press of America.

Freire, P. (1995). *Pedagogy of the oppressed.* New York, NY: Continuum.

Gecan, M. (2002). *Going public.* Boston, MA: Beacon Press.

Gergen, K. J. (1995). Relational theory and the discourses of power. In D. M. Hosking & H. P. Dachler (Eds.), *Management and organization: Relational alternatives to individualism* (pp. 29–49). Aldershot, UK: Avebury Press. Retrieved from https://www.academia.edu/2630295/Relational_theory_and_the_discourses_of_power

Giroux, H. (2015). *Higher education and the politics of disruption.* Retrieved from http://philosophersforchange.org/2015/03/24/higher-education-and-the-politics-of-disruption/

Gordon, L. (2014, September 15). USC unveiling plans for $650-million housing, retail complex. *Los Angeles Times.* Retrieved from http://www.latimes.com/local/education/la-me-usc-village-20140915-story.html

Gottlieb, J. (1999, November 30). The big business of college "naming opportunities." *Los Angeles Times.* Retrieved from http://articles.latimes.com/1999/nov/30/news/mn-38984

Guillen, F. (2012). Including Latino communities in the learning process: Curricular and pedagogical reforms in undergraduate Spanish programs. *Journal of Community Engagement and Scholarship, 3*(2). Retrieved from http://jces.ua.edu/including-latino-communities-in-the-learning-process-curricular-and-pedagogical-reforms-in-undergraduate-spanish-programs/

Heldman, C. (2011). Solidarity, not charity: Issues of privilege in service-learning. In M. Cress & D. M. Donahue (Eds.), *Democratic dilemmas in teaching service-learning: Curricular strategies for success* (pp. 33–42). Sterling, VA: Stylus.

Horton, M., & Freire, P. (1990). *We make the road by walking: Conversations on education and social change.* Philadelphia, PA: Temple University Press.

Imagining America. (n.d.). *About.* Retrieved from http://imaginingamerica.org/about/our-mission/

Industrial Areas Foundation. (2017). *Training information.* Retrieved from http://www.industrialareasfoundation.org/training

Jacoby, B. (2003). *Building partnerships for service-learning.* San Francisco, CA: Jossey-Bass.

Kezar, A. (2012). *Embracing non-tenure track faculty.* New York, NY: Routledge.

Kezar, A., & Maxey, D. (2015). *Adapting by design: Creating faculty roles and defining faculty work to ensure an intentional future for colleges and universities.* Retrieved from https://www.insidehighered.com/sites/default/server_files/files/DELPHI%20PROJECT_ADAPTINGBYDESIGN_EMBARGOED%20(1).pdf

King, M. L. (1967). *Where do we go from here?* Retrieved from http://kingencyclopedia.stanford.edu/encyclopedia/documentsentry/where_do_we_go_from_here_delivered_at_the_11th_annual_sclc_convention/

Koritz, A., & Sanchez, J. (2009). *Civic engagement in the wake of Katrina.* Ann Arbor: University of Michigan Press.

Ledwith, M., & Springett, J. (2010). *Participatory practice: Community-based action for transformative change.* Portland, OR: The Policy Press.

Lynch, K. (2008, May). International league tables and rankings in higher education: An appraisal. *Level3,* (6). Retrieved from http://level3.dit.ie/html/issue6/lynch/lynch.pdf

Lynton, E. (1983). A crisis of purpose: Reexamining the role of the university. *Change, 15,* 18–23, 53.

Mankiller, W. (1993). *Mankiller: A chief and her people.* New York, NY: St. Martin's Press.

Maurrasse, D. J. (2001). *Beyond the campus: How colleges and universities form partnerships with their communities.* New York, NY: Routledge.

McIlrath, L., Lyons, A., & Munck, R. (2012). *Higher education and civic engagement: comparative perspectives.* New York, NY: Palgrave MacMillan.

Mezirow, J. (1990). *Fostering critical reflection in adulthood: A guide to transformative and emancipatory learning.* San Francisco, CA: Jossey-Bass.

Minkler, M., & Wallerstein, N. (2011). Improving health through community organization and community building. In M. Minkler (Ed.), *Community organizing and community building for health* (pp. 26–50). New Brunswick, NJ: Rutgers University Press.

Munck, R., McIlrath, L., Hall, B., & Tandon, R. (2014). *Higher education and community-based research: Creating a global vision.* New York, NY: Palgrave Macmillan.

New England Resource Center for Higher Education. (n.d.). *Carnegie community engagement classification.* Retrieved from http://nerche.org/index .php?option=com_content&view=article&id=341&Itemid=618#NERCHECF

Newfield, C. (2011). *Unmaking the public university: The forty-year assault on the middle class.* Cambridge, MA: Harvard University Press.

Nohria, N., & Khurana, R. (2010). *Handbook of leadership theory and practice: A Harvard Business School centennial colloquium.* Cambridge, MA: Harvard Business School.

Occidental College. (n.d.). *Committees.* Retrieved from http://www.oxy.edu/faculty/ faculty-council/committees

Organisation for Economic Co-operation and Development. (1996). *The knowledge-based economy.* Paris, France: Author. Retrieved from https://www .oecd.org/sti/sci-tech/1913021.pdf

Ospina, S., & Foldy, E. (2010). Building bridges from the margins: The work of leadership in social change organizations. *The Leadership Quarterly, 21,* 292–307.

Osterman, P. (2002). *Gathering power: The future of progressive politics in America.* Boston, MA: Beacon Press.

Payne, C. M. (1995/2007). *I've got the light of freedom: The organizing tradition and the Mississippi freedom struggle.* Berkeley: University of California Press.

Peters, S. J. (2010). *Democracy and higher education: Traditions and stories of civic engagement.* East Lansing: Michigan State University Press.

Peters, S., & Avila, M. (2014). Organizing culture change through community-based research. In R. Munck, L. McIlrath, B. Hall, & R. Tandon (Eds.), *Higher education and community-based research: Creating a global vision* (pp. 133–147). New York, NY: Palgrave Macmillan.

President's Commission on Higher Education. (1948). *Higher education for American democracy: A report of the President's Commission on Higher Education.* New York, NY: Harper & Brothers.

Rappaport, J. (1984). Studies in empowerment: Introduction to the issue. *Prevention in Human Services, 3(2/3),* 1–7.

Reciprocity. (2017). In *English Oxford living dictionaries.* Retrieved from http:// www.oxforddictionaries.com/us/definition/american_english/reciprocity

Rogers, M. B. (1990). *Cold anger: A story of faith and power politics*. Denton: University of North Texas Press.

Rudd, M. (2013). How to build a movement: Activism vs. organizing. *The North Star*. Retrieved from http://www.thenorthstar.info/?p=9474

Ryan, A. B. (2001). *Feminist ways of knowing: Towards theorising the person for radical adult education*. Leicester, Ireland: National Institute of Adult Continuing Education.

Saltmarsh, J., & Hartley, M. (2012). *To serve a larger purpose: Engagement for democracy and the transformation of higher education*. Philadelphia, PA: Temple University Press.

Snyder-Hall, C. (2013). *Civic aspirations: Why some higher education faculty are reconnecting their professional and public lives*. Dayton, OH: Kettering Foundation.

Stanton, T., Giles, D., & Cruz, N. I. (1999). *Service-learning: A movement's pioneers reflect on its origins, practice, and future*. San Francisco, CA: Jossey-Bass.

Stoecker, R., & Tryon, E. A. (2009). *The unheard voices: Community organizations and service-learning*. Philadelphia, PA: Temple University Press.

Strand, K., Marullo, S. Cutforth, N., Stoecker, R., & Donohue, P. (2003). *Community-based research and higher education*. San Francisco, CA: Jossey-Bass.

Texas Archival Resources Online. (n.d.). *A guide to the industrial areas foundation records*. Retrieved from https://www.lib.utexas.edu/taro/utcah/00172/cah-00172.html

University of Georgia. *Guidelines for appointment, promotion and tenure*. Approved by the University Council on April 22, 2004. Revised by the University Council 2006, 2007, 2010 and 2011, 2013 and 2014. Retrieved from http://provost.uga.edu/documents/guidenlines_revised_spring_14.pdf

Wallerstein, N. (1992). Powerlessness, empowerment, and health: Implications for health promotion programs. *American Journal of Health Promotion, 6*, 197–205.

Warden, R. (2014). Rewarding academics for civic engagement gains ground. *University World News, 335*. Retrieved from http://www.universityworldnews.com/article.php?story=2014091807261155

Wheeler, K. H. (2011). *Cultivating regionalism: Higher education and the making of the American Midwest*. DeKalb: Northern Illinois University Press.

Wolin, S. S. (1989). *The presence of the past: Essays on the state and the Constitution*. Baltimore, MD: Johns Hopkins University Press.

Zlotkowski, E. A. (1998). *Successful service-learning programs: New models of excellence in higher education*. Bolton, MA: Anker.

ABOUT THE AUTHOR

Maria Avila is a faculty member in the Master of Social Work program at the California State University, Dominguez Hills. She is a member of Imagining America National Advisory Board. Avila's research focuses on participatory action research with faculty and with community partners and is aimed at creating democratic, civic engagement inside and outside of higher education institutions.

She was the director of the Center for Community-Based Learning at Occidental College from 2001 to 2011, having earlier worked as a community organizer and a social worker in Mexico and in the United States for more than 20 years.

Prior to working in higher education, Avila was a community organizer with the Industrial Areas Foundation, the international network founded by the late Saul D. Alinksy in the 1940s. She has performed volunteer and consulting work with a number of organizations, including Partnerships to Uplift Communities, the Northeast LA Education Strategy, the City of Los Angeles, Imagining America: Artists and Scholars in Public Life, and the Council for Social Work Education's Council on Global Issues.

Avila has given numerous talks and workshops in the topics of civic engagement and community organizing at national and international conferences and venues and has published several book chapters and journal articles.

INDEX